by
Beatrice Hughes

Quilted Star and Logo Banner

For Organizations and Individuals with a Big Ten Affiliation

And Anyone Interested in Making an Eleven-Point Star
Where Each Point has Two Colors

From Concept
To
Completion

Editors
Sally Pratt, PhD
Katherine Mervau, C.P.S.

Photography
Banner on book cover: MSU Museum/Pearl Yee Wong
Photos in book: Beatrice Hughes

Illustrations
Beatrice Hughes

Hughes, Beatrice Carol Knight
        Quilted Star and Logo Banner
Summary: Quiltmaking design process and construction using pattern pieces and techniques developed for making an eleven-point star. Each star point contains two colors. Step-by-step instructions utilize 150 drawings and 58 photos plus helpful tips for making this project.

Full — (Circle) — Publications

1261 Cambria Drive
East Lansing, MI 48823

Library of Congress Control Number 2008944196

ISBN 978-0-615-27065-4

Manufactured in the United States of America

Copyright © 2008 Author, Beatrice Hughes

A fabric kit is available to make this project.
To purchase additional books, a fabric kit or a Big Ten pin collection,
e-mail starandlogobanner@comcast.net
or use the order form at the back of this book

Dedication

Attention to detail is part of my inherent makeup. Instilled in me by the Almighty, I am thankful for that gift.

To Harold, my loving husband, who encourages me in quilting activities.

To all the quilters that have added zest to my life.

Acknowledgements

Arlene Brophy, a member of the Michigan State University Community Club, visited the MSUCC Quilting Interest Group. She brought her collection of Big Ten university lapel pins asking for some tips on how to display them on a banner for use at MSUCC meetings. The quilting group agreed to come up with some concepts. Her visit led to not only a banner, but also a note card based on the banner, this book and a banner fabric kit. I thank her for her query.

After volunteering to develop some designs, The MSUCC Quilting Interest Group gave me the thumbs-up to develop designs for a display banner featuring the lapel pins. I valued their confidence in my skills.

I greatly appreciated all the help and input, which Joan Gilliland gave me while working on this project. She immediately volunteered to work with me in the process of finalizing the design, selecting fabrics, preparing and cutting fabrics and completing some final sewing steps. Her input was invaluable. Thank you. Thank you. Thank you.

Thanks go to the Michigan State University Community Club Board, that approved funding for both the banner project and the note card project.

Sally Pratt, PhD and Katherine Mervau, C.P.S. both get big accolades for editing this manuscript. They did it on short notice and in short order. Thank you both.

Martha Schwab, Molly Green Haywood and Joan Gilliland gave me invaluable tweaks for the cover.

Thanks to all for their part in this process.

Contents

A Few Favorite Brands

3M
Avery
Corner Mark-It
Dritz
Fiskars
General's
Gingher
Griffin
Hewlett-Packard
Hobbs Bonded Fibers
Mark-B-Gone
Mountain Mist
Niagara
Nikon
Olfa
Omnigrid
Prym
Quilter's Rule
Singer

Eleven Fun Facts

1. An 11 sided polygon is called a hendecagon.
2. The United States Susan B. Anthony dollar is 11 sided.
3. The Canadian one dollar coin is 11 sided and clocks depicted on Canadian currency point to 11 o'clock.
4. The average adult male heart weighs 11 ounces.
5. Apollo 11 made the first lunar landing.
6. One of the prime numbers is 11.
7. American football, soccer, cricket, and field hockey are all played with teams of 11 players on the field.
8. A rugby ball is 11 inches long.
9. The space shuttle went up on its 11th mission, weighing 11 tons and fixed an errant satellite on the 11th day of the 11th month.
10. World War I ended on the 11th hour of the 11th day of the 11th month.
11. Both television shows Cheers and MASH ran for 11 seasons with 11 main characters.

Introduction and Project Description

Eleven-Point Star in a Hendecagon

Designed for the Michigan State University Community Club, this banner expresses affiliation between the organization and Michigan State University, and it expresses a wider affiliation with other academia that make up the Big Ten (currently eleven universities).

The project is an eleven-point star. Each two-color star point represents the colors of one university that make up part of the Big Ten Conference. The star sits in a hendecagon, the name of an eleven-sided polygon.

The pattern is designed to distribute university colors evenly. Even though the MSU colors are shown at the top of this design, any of the university colors can be rotated to the top.

Eleven is an unusual number with which to work. It is also unusual to see a finely pointed two-color star point. The angle of rotation for each star point is 32.7272... degrees. The pattern and process described in this book makes it easy for others to work with this atypical star arrangement.

A primary design aspect is to display each university's pin on one banner. You can collect these pins at individual university bookstores, at sporting events and on the Internet. The pins add interest

and sprit. Examples of the pins are included in the materials.

A feature that enhances the multi-color star points is the inclusion of the organization's logo in the center of the polygon. The logo, printed on a computer printer fabric sheet, is in the banner's center. The logo could also be added using a copy center's services or by embroidery.

This quilted banner design is for sewers, designers, quilters and others interested in making an eleven-point star. Construction involves techniques employed in those fields.

To display the 20" wide by 28" long banner, hang it on a podium, from a table, on a banner stand or on a wall.

All the pattern pieces and a description of each step used to make this project are included in this book. A list of supplies and a list of tools are included. Use the pattern pieces at the end of the book for precise cutting of the fabric.

Supplies

Eleven University Pins – Lapel size – one from each Big Ten university

Logo Hendecagon – One inkjet computer printer fabric sheet – ColorTextiles and Printed Treasures are good brands

Copy of organization's logo

Fabrics – all 100% Cotton
   Wing parts A – 1/4 yard neutral (darkest shade of three neutrals used)

   Wing parts B – Medium neutral shade of three neutrals used – see background fabric requirements below

   Wing Parts C – 1/2 yard neutral (lightest shade of three neutrals to be used)

   Background – 2 yards of neutral used also for the medium shade on Wing parts B
   There are layout directions for 44" wide fabric and fabric that is less than 44" wide.

   University Colors for Outside Left and Right Star Points
      White – 1/4 yard of closely woven fabric (used for four of the universities)
      Black – 1/4 yard (used for two of the universities)
      All other university colors – sixteen 1/4 yard pieces – one for each of the remaining university colors (refer to the university color page that follows)

   Inside Triangular Star Points – included in the university colors above

   Backing Fabric – included in the background yardage

   Binding and Sleeves – included in the background yardage

Batting – Craft size batting 34" x 45" – batting should be a thin type
Hobbs Bonded Thermore, Mountain Mist Cream Rose and Warm and Natural for example

Paper – Craft or drawing paper 26" x 30" or larger used for drawing background pattern

Glue stick – water soluble made for using with fabrics

Other – A wood or metal curtain rod and decorative cord for hanging, 3/4 yard rope type drapery weights for bottom, two tassels. These are available at fabric and home decoration stores.

Fabric Preparation
      Launder all fabrics by color. Wash in hot water. Rinse in cold water with fabric softener added. Check for color bleeding. Wash until bleeding stops. Discard any fabric that continues to bleed. You do not want your white fabrics to turn pink, blue or another color after your project is completed and laundered.

      Dry until damp.

      Iron all wrinkles while completing the drying process.

      Starch each piece before cutting pattern pieces. Starching improves accuracy when cutting and sewing, makes it easier to press seams open and helps prevent raveling. When rinsing out blue markings, added before the quilting process, the starch and blue markings come out in the final rinsing step.

Tools

Rotary cutting mats – Olfa or another brand – preferably two 24" x 36" grids aligned and boards taped together

Rotary cutter

New rotary cutter blade(s)

Omnigrid ruler to use with mat and cutter 3" x 18"

Quilter's Ruler (or similar rotary cutting ruler) 6-1/2" x 24"

Straight edge at least 36" long – a metal yardstick works well

Yardstick compass points – Made by Griffin and available through Blick Art Materials
Their web site is: www.dickblick.com/zz554/33/. They are also available in some catalogs, quilting, craft and art supply stores. You will also need a yardstick or long straight piece of wood that fits the opening in each compass point, which houses the yardstick.

Electric illuminated light table – a light bulb under a glass top table also works

Scissors – sewing to snip threads
        A pair to cut paper pattern pieces but a rotary cutter is preferred for this process

Sewing machine
        Machine needles – size 11/80
        1/4" Presser foot
        Other machine supplies such as a magnifying glass or tools you typically like to use when sewing
        Foot used for machine quilting

Thread – beige colors to blend with background and other neutral fabrics
        Various color to blend with star point colors

Prym brand water soluble fabric glue stick

Dritz brand Fray Check

Fine silk straight pins

Medium-size safety pins for pinning banner layers together before quilting

Sewing needles

Mark-B-Gone brand fine-point blue, water-soluble pen

Fine point white pencil – preferably General brand #4414

Pencil sharpener that makes a good, sharp point

Sticky labels for labeling banner sections before sewing

Iron with steam feature

Spray starch – Niagara brand

Medium weight terry cloth bath towel used for covering ironing board while using spray starch

Spray water bottle that delivers a fine mist

Computer, scanner, printer, software for printing your organization logo on fabric

Corner Mark-It ruler for mitering binding corners

Color Key

Indiana University — Cream, Crimson

Michigan State University — Green, White

Northwestern University — Royal Purple, White

Ohio State University — Scarlet, Gray

Pennsylvania State University — Blue, White

Purdue University — Old Gold, Black

University of Illinois at Urbana-Champaign — Orange, Blue

University of Iowa — Black, Gold

The University of Michigan — Maize, Blue

University of Minnesota, Twin Cities — Maroon, Gold

University of Wisconsin-Madison — Cardinal, White

University Pin Examples

Indiana
University

Michigan State
University

Northwestern
University

Ohio State
University

Pennsylvania
State University

Purdue
University

University of
Illinois at
Urbana-
Champaign

University of
Iowa

The University
of Michigan

University of
Minnesota,
Twin Cities

University of
Wisconsin-
Madison

Pattern Pieces

The banner is made up of eight pattern pieces as follows:

Pieces:

A = the darkest shade wing part

B = the medium shade wing part

C = the lightest shade wing part

Right Outside Star Point

Left Outside Star Point

Inside Triangular Star Point

Logo Hendecagon

Background

University Pins
An alternate location is outside the
star within the background quilting
pattern, as shown on the book
cover.

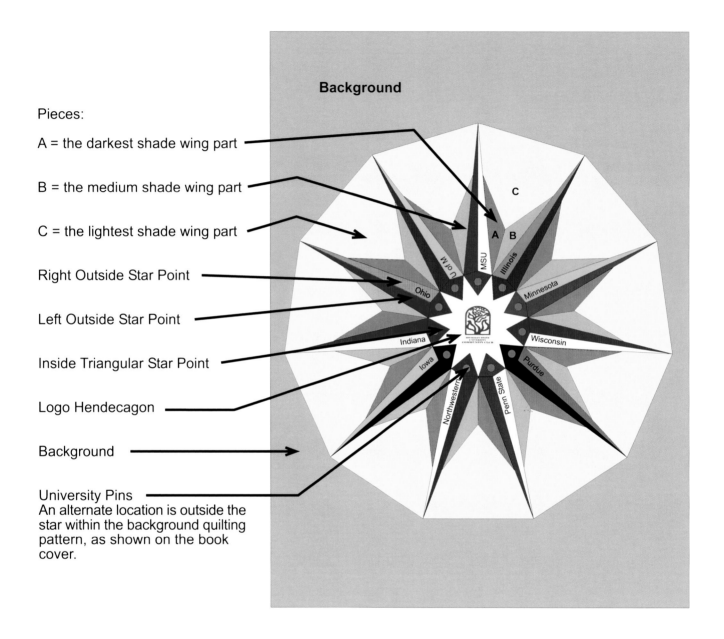

The Background pattern is made from directions and a page called the Hendecagon Page. The remaining pattern pieces are supplied. An extra set of pattern pieces is included at the back.

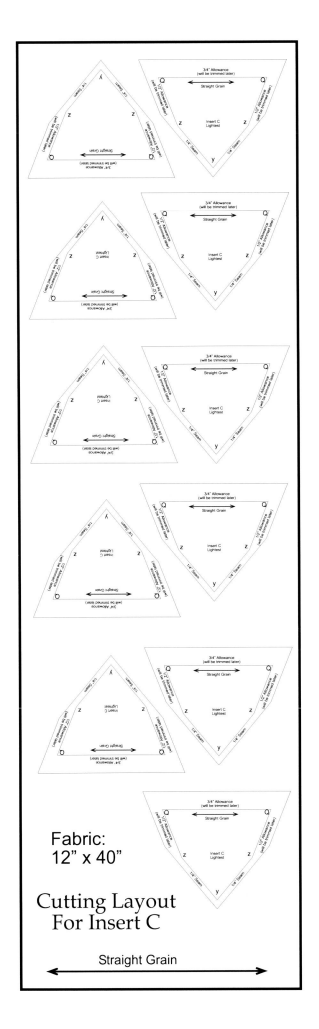

Fabric:
12" x 40"

Cutting Layout
For Insert C

Straight Grain

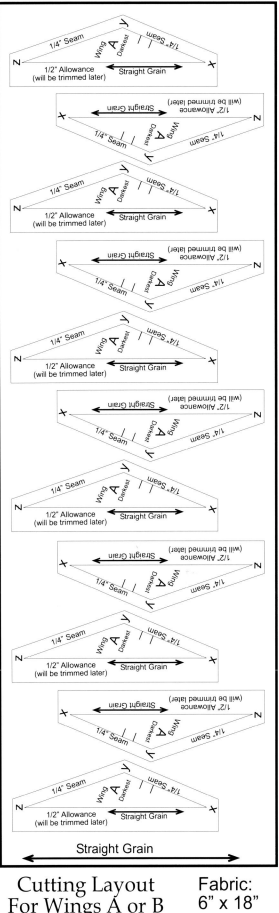

Straight Grain

Cutting Layout
For Wings A or B

Fabric:
6" x 18"

Star Points
Cutting Guide

WHITE FABRIC

Fabric required: 1/4 yard (actual equals 1/4 yard long by 8" wide)

Be sure to place pattern pieces on straight grain of fabric as indicated. Place on right side of fabric.

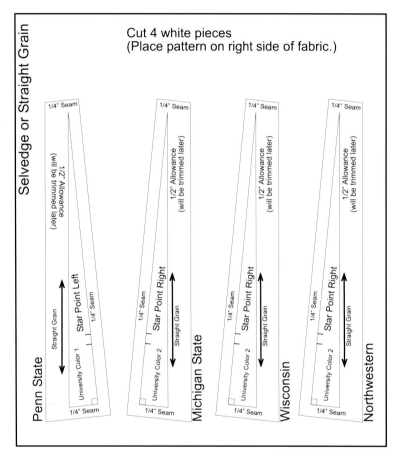

BLACK FABRIC

Fabric required 1/4 yard (actual equals 1/4 yard long by 4" wide)

Be sure to place pattern pieces on straight grain of fabric as indicated. Place on right side of fabric.

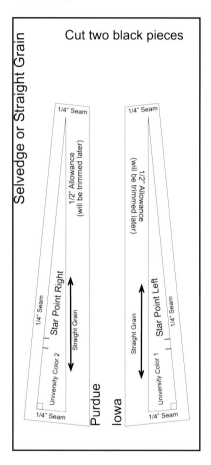

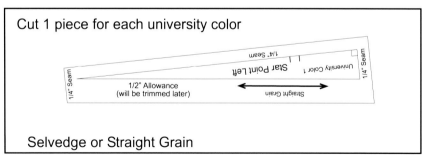

REMAINING COLORS (other than white and black)

Fabric required 1/4 yard (actual equals 1/4 yard long by 3" wide)

Be sure to place pattern pieces on straight grain of fabric. Also place on right side of fabric. NOTE: Some pattern pieces will need to be for the RIGHT star point and some will need to be for the LEFT star point. CHECK THIS AGAINST the color illustrated banner BEFORE CUTTING

Background, Backing, Binding Wings B and Sleeves

Cutting Guide

Shown below are two variations for cutting the two yards of fabric used for the Background, Backing, Binding, Wing Parts B and the two sleeves.

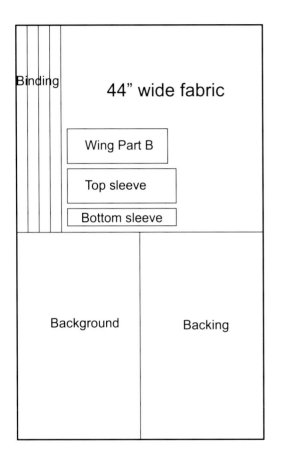

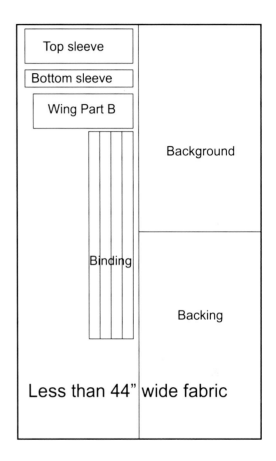

Inside Triangular Star Point

Cutting Guide

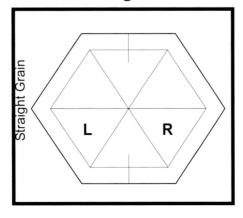

Fabric required
3-1/2" wide x 3" high
of each 11 colors

9

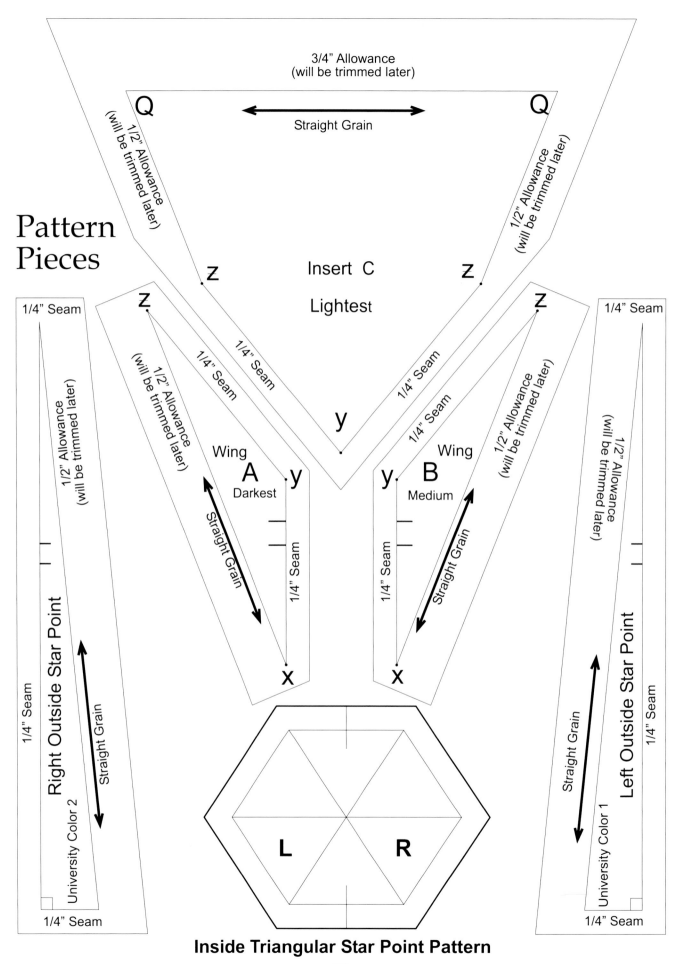

Pattern Pieces

3/4" Allowance
(will be trimmed later)

Q
Straight Grain
Q

1/2" Allowance
(will be trimmed later)

1/2" Allowance
(will be trimmed later)

z

Insert C

z

Lightest

1/4" Seam

1/4" Seam

z

z

1/4" Seam

1/4" Seam

1/4" Seam

1/2" Allowance
(will be trimmed later)

1/4" Seam

1/2" Allowance
(will be trimmed later)

y

1/4" Seam

1/4" Seam

Wing

Wing

A

B

Darkest

Medium

1/2" Allowance
(will be trimmed later)

1/2" Allowance
(will be trimmed later)

Straight Grain

y

Straight Grain

y

1/4" Seam

1/4" Seam

1/4" Seam

1/4" Seam

1/4" Seam

1/2" Allowance
(will be trimmed later)

1/2" Allowance
(will be trimmed later)

Right Outside Star Point

Left Outside Star Point

Straight Grain

Straight Grain

University Color 2

University Color 1

x

x

1/4" Seam

1/4" Seam

1/4" Seam

1/4" Seam

L

R

Inside Triangular Star Point Pattern

10

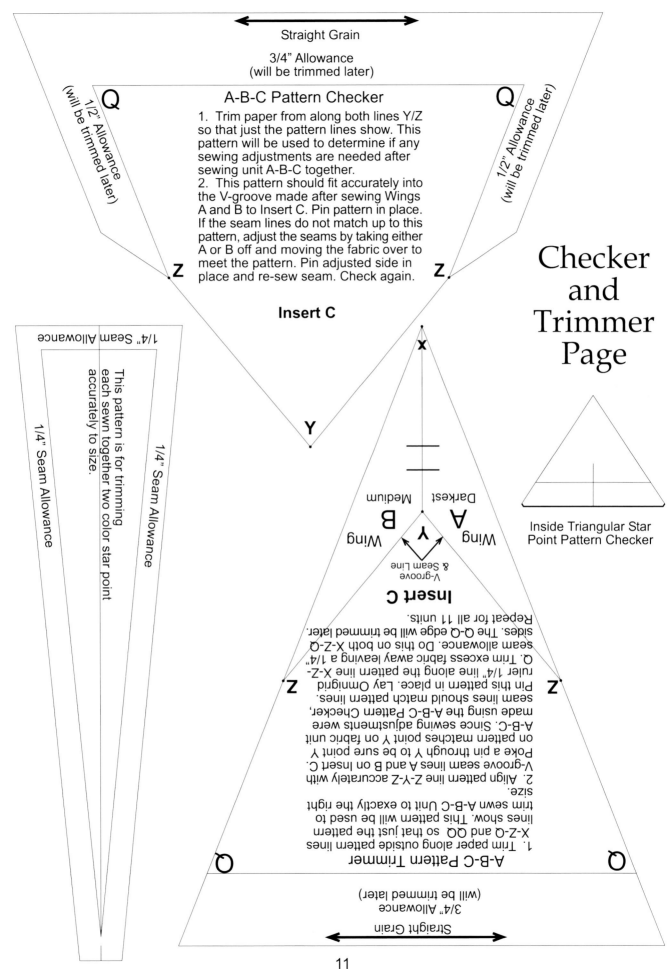

Straight Grain

3/4" Allowance
(will be trimmed later)

A-B-C Pattern Checker

1. Trim paper from along both lines Y/Z so that just the pattern lines show. This pattern will be used to determine if any sewing adjustments are needed after sewing unit A-B-C together.

2. This pattern should fit accurately into the V-groove made after sewing Wings A and B to Insert C. Pin pattern in place. If the seam lines do not match up to this pattern, adjust the seams by taking either A or B off and moving the fabric over to meet the pattern. Pin adjusted side in place and re-sew seam. Check again.

Insert C

Q

Q

1/2" Allowance
(will be trimmed later)

1/2" Allowance
(will be trimmed later)

Z

Z

X

Y

Inside Triangular Star
Point Pattern Checker

Darkest

Medium

A Wing

B Wing

Y

V-groove
& Seam Line

Insert C

Repeat for all 11 units.

A-B-C Pattern Trimmer

1. Trim paper along outside pattern lines X-Z-Q and QQ so that just the pattern lines show. This pattern will be used to trim sewn A-B-C Unit to exactly the right size.

2. Align pattern line Z-Y-Z accurately with V-groove seam lines A and B on Insert C. Poke a pin through Y to be sure point Y on pattern matches point Y on fabric unit A-B-C. Since sewing adjustments were made using the A-B-C Pattern Checker, seam lines should match pattern lines. Pin this pattern in place. Lay Omnigrid ruler 1/4" line along the pattern line X-Z-Q. Trim excess fabric away leaving a 1/4" seam allowance. Do this on both X-Z-Q sides. The Q-Q edge will be trimmed later.

Z

Z

Q

Q

3/4" Allowance
(will be trimmed later)

Straight Grain

1/4" Seam Allowance

This pattern is for trimming each sewn together two color star point accurately to size.

1/4" Seam Allowance

1/4" Seam Allowance

Center Hendecagon Pattern

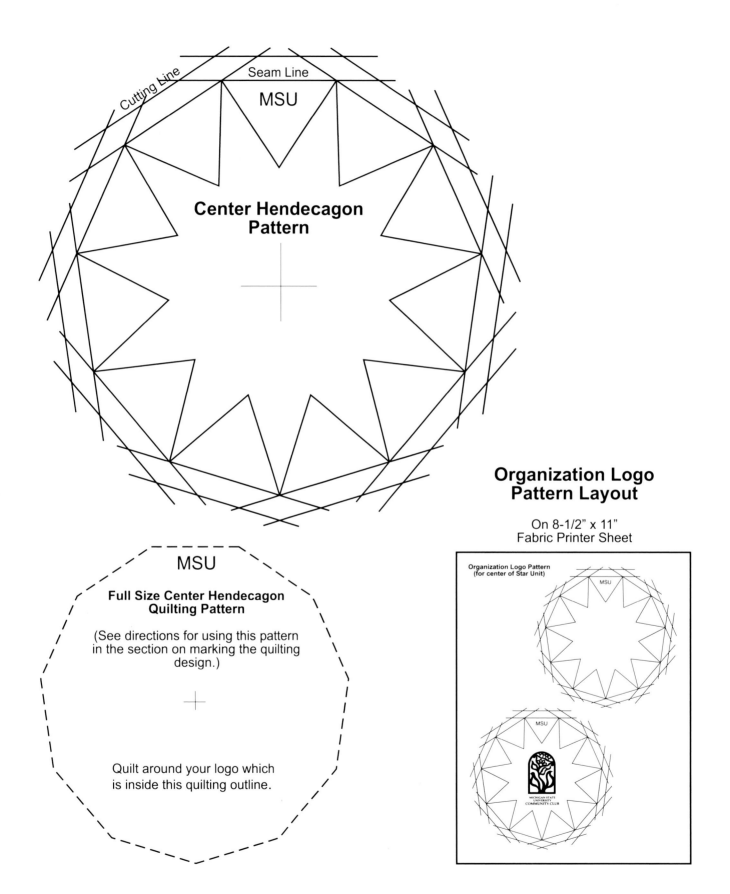

Cutting Line

Seam Line

MSU

**Center Hendecagon
Pattern**

MSU

**Full Size Center Hendecagon
Quilting Pattern**

(See directions for using this pattern
in the section on marking the quilting
design.)

Quilt around your logo which
is inside this quilting outline.

**Organization Logo
Pattern Layout**

On 8-1/2" x 11"
Fabric Printer Sheet

Organization Logo Pattern
(for center of Star Unit)

MSU

MSU

MICHIGAN STATE
UNIVERSITY
COMMUNITY CLUB

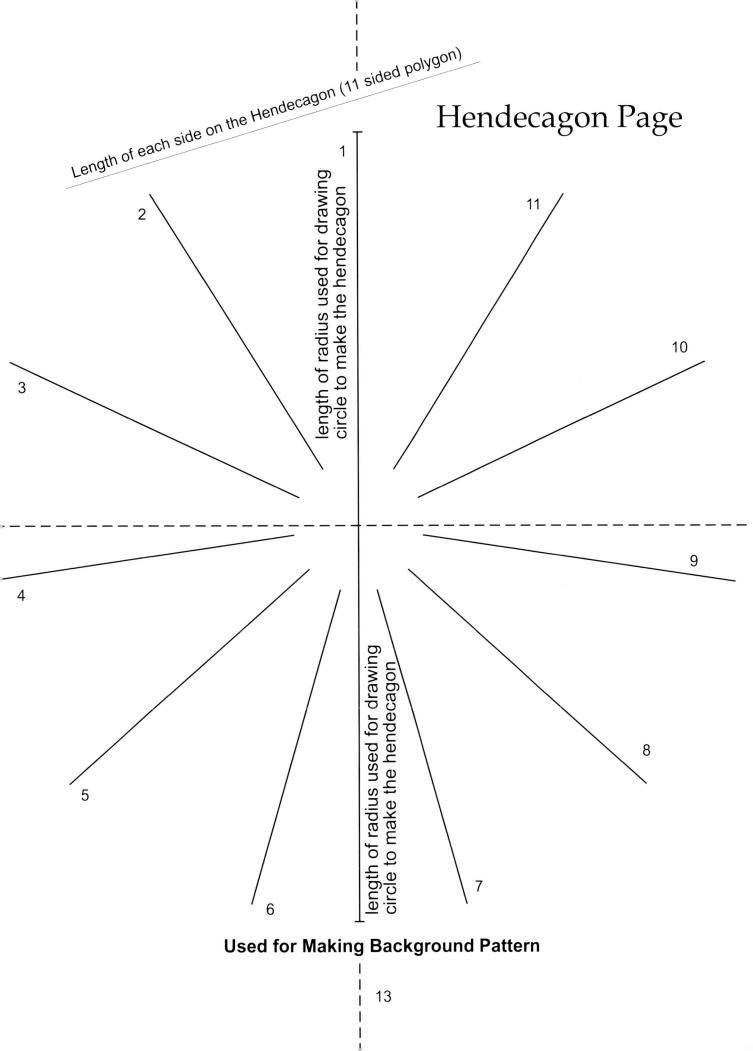

Hendecagon Page

Length of each side on the Hendecagon (11 sided polygon)

length of radius used for drawing circle to make the hendecagon

1

2

3

4

5

6

7

8

9

10

11

length of radius used for drawing circle to make the hendecagon

Used for Making Background Pattern

13

Project Notes

Made by _____

Date Started _____

Notes on Process

_____

_____

_____

_____

_____

_____

_____

Date Finished _____

Construction

Wings A and B and Insert C

Cutting Insert C

Insert C is the lightest shade of the A-B-C Unit colors. Use the full size Insert C pattern pieces at the end of the book. The patterns are for both cutting the fabric and for sewing. Cut out each pattern piece along the outside line. Use a rotary cutter to do this. Leave the cutting line so that it just shows. The Cutting Layout for pattern C is on page 7. Pin the pattern pieces to the fabric placing patterns on straight grain as noted. Cut each out. Leave the Insert C pattern pieces pinned to the fabric.

Cutting Wings A and B

Wing A is the darkest shade of the two wing colors. Wing B is the medium shade of the two wing colors. Use the page 7 cutting layout for these wing sections. Both A and B have the same layout. Pin the patterns in place according to the straight grain designation. Cut the wings according to the color designation.

Sewing

Turn Insert C over so that pattern is on bottom as shown (upper right photo), leave pattern pinned to the fabric. Look closely at photo. One pin is visible.

The first photo at the right also shows wing pattern pieces A (darkest shade) and B (medium shade) on top of their respective fabrics.

Switch A and B pattern pieces so that A is on the back of Wing B fabric and B is on back of A Wing fabric. They are the same size and shape. Pin patterns in place.

This is done so that Y and Z points can be seen when matching wing points to those on Insert C.

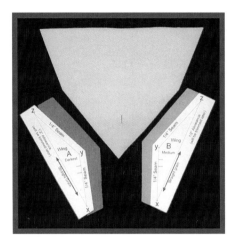

Lay right side (not direction left and right but right side as opposed to wrong side) of darkest wing fabric against right side of Insert C fabric. Match points Z and Y on B and C pieces by poking a pin through the respective pattern points and pinning in place.

Remove the pins from Wing pattern except at points Z and Y.

As shown in the photo below, lift wing pattern and pin wing fabric to Insert C fabric and pattern as shown. Remove pins that were placed at points Y and Z and remove wing pattern. Turn unit to pattern side of Insert C.

15

As shown in the next photo, put sewing machine needle into Insert C pattern and fabric layers at point Z. Stitch forward two or three stitches. Then back-stitch to point Z. Then sew forward on seam line, stitch toward Y. Stop at point Y. Backstitch 3 to 4 stitches.

Pin and sew second wing in the same way keeping first wing out of the way of the stitching.

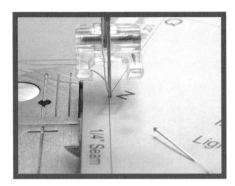

With Insert C pattern piece still in place, fold C in half lengthwise down center as shown. Pin A and B Wings together along XY side where the // hatch marks are.

Stitch a 1/4" seam from raw edge by X (with a backstitch) and stitch to Y. Stop at Y. Do not cross the stitching where A and B were sewn to C. Backstitch to secure the point at Y.

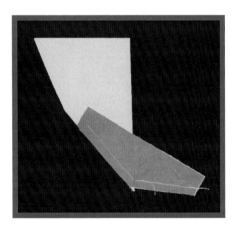

Sewing of the first A-B-C Unit is now complete. The remaining A-B-C Units are sewn in the same way.

Carefully remove pattern C. It helps to fold the pattern along the stitching line perforated by the sewing machine needle. The unit with the pattern removed is shown in the photo at the top right.

The unit is ready to be pressed.

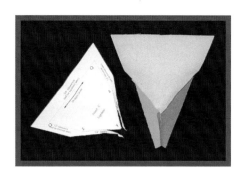

Pressing

With the unit's right side against an ironing surface, press seam XY (the one down the center of AB Wings) open.

Press the seams on C toward AB Wings. Turn over and press the right side of the unit.

The photo below shows the wrong side of unit A-B-C. The black lines drawn on the photo help make the raw edges of the seams visible and a dashed line shows the stitching line on Insert C.

Spray starch and then iron the seams to help keep them in place and flat.

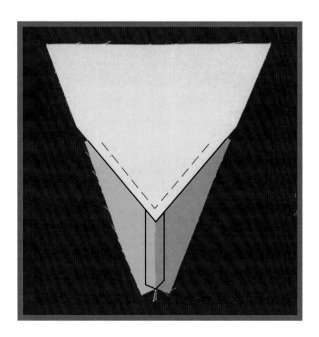

Each A-B-C Unit is pressed in the same way.

The A-B-C Units are ready for the checking step

Checking A-B-C Unit Size

Checking sewing accuracy in an intricate pattern is an important step to a satisfactory finished project. Eleven accurate A-B-C wedges are easier to work with, and a process to check for any changes needed is included here.

The **Checker and Trimmer Page** shows two slightly modified patterns. One pattern is called the **A-B-C Pattern Checker**. Use a rotary cuter and cut out the pattern according to the directions on it. Leave the 1/2" and 3/4" seam allowances attached to the trimmed pattern. Be sure the seam line between ZYZ just shows.

Using the A-B-C Pattern Checker

This pattern should fit accurately into the V-groove made after sewing Wings A and B to Insert C. Slide the point at Y onto the sewn A-B-C Unit. Check to see if it fits.

Check and Adjust

Pin A-B-C Pattern Checker to the A-B-C fabric unit. Be sure pattern edges align with seam line.

In the close-up example below, the seam line of Wing A does not align and needs adjusting.

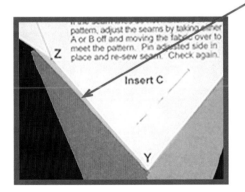

Make adjustments as described below

Take out the stitches along YZ seam that needs adjusting and move the wing against the pattern. On the right side, pin the wing in place so that it can be folded back and re-sewn.

On the wrong side, re-pin wing and sew seam again. Stitch the wing along the pressed fold of the Wing A seam.

After adjusting and re-sewing, check to be sure the A-B-C Pattern Checker fits snugly into the V-groove of the A-B-C Unit.

Shown below is the re-sewn unit with a good fit.

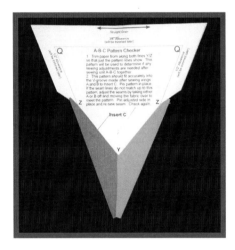

Test fit on all eleven A-B-C Units and adjust fit as necessary.

The A-B-C Units are ready to be trimmed to size.

Trimming A-B-C Unit to Size

Sewing inherently reduces fabric dimension at seam lines. Allowing extra fabric on outside edges allows for trimming after a unit is sewn together. The extra fabric is an important attribute when completing a hendecagon with thin star points. The extra fabric allows for trimming and more accuracy as each step progresses.

The outside seams of A B and C were cut at 1/2". The following steps will progress through the A-B-C Unit trimming process.

The **Checker and Trimmer Page** shows two slightly modified patterns. One pattern is called the **A-B-C Pattern Trimmer**. Cut out the pattern according to the directions on it. Be sure to leave the 3/4" seam allowance showing. It will be trimmed later.

Put a couple layers of Scotch tape on the front and back of the pattern over point Y to stabilize the pattern and keep the pattern from ripping when pinning into point Y. An illuminated light table makes the following pinning process much easier.

Using the A-B-C Pattern Trimmer

Lay the Pattern Trimmer on top of the <u>back</u> of the A-B-C fabric unit.

Pin the A-B-C Pattern Trimmer to the sewn fabric pieces. Begin by matching point Y on the pattern to the corresponding Y area on the fabric unit. Pin through all layers. Pin at point X and both Z points as well. Also pin along the top of the pattern near QQ. Double check that all areas are in their respective places. See the next photo.

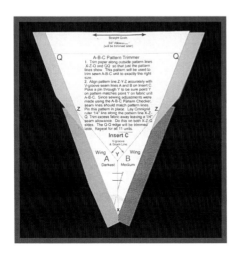

The Pattern Trimmer is shown pinned to the fabric. Each point, X, Y and Z of the pattern are aligned with those respective placement points on the fabric

Below are close up pictures of where each point needs to align.

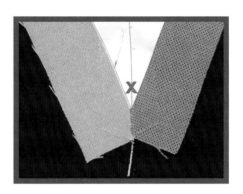

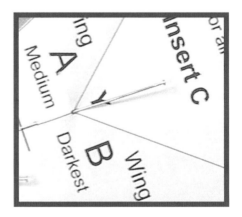

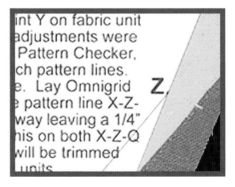

Trimming

Lay an Omnigrid quilting ruler 1/4" line along the pattern line X-Z-Q. Hold ruler securely and trim the excess fabric away using a rotary cutter leaving a 1/4" seam allowance. Trim on both sides.

Trim all eleven A-B-C Units in the same way.

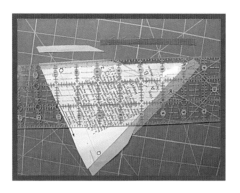

The photo above shows that the first side is trimmed along the ruler edge.

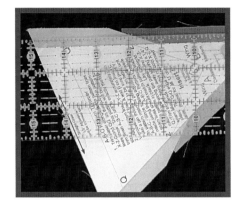

Above, the photo shows the ruler alignment.

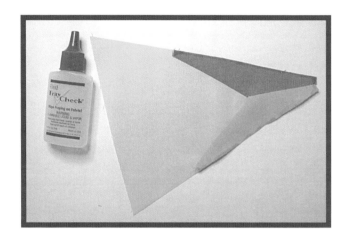

Shown above is a finished A-B-C Unit. Sewing is adjusted and the unit is trimmed to size.

To stabilize the sides Fray Check all edges of all A-B-C Units after trimming. Be sure to only put a narrow bead of Fray Check along edges so that it does not spread beyond the 1/4" seam allowance. Remember, the 3/4" side will be trimmed later and may be uneven.

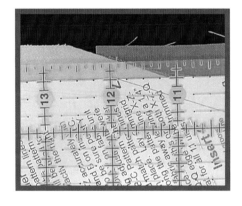

This photo is a close-up that shows the ruler alignment on the first side.

Construction
Outside Two-Color Star Points

Fabric Choices

Each of the eleven universities in the Big Ten has a specific pair of official school colors as described on page 4, the color key page. Four schools have white as one of the colors and these four pattern pieces can be cut from the same white fabric. Two schools have black as one of the official colors and these two pattern pieces can be cut from the same black fabric. The remaining pattern pieces for the star points are cut from specific colors of fabric chosen to represent each particular school.

The sewing directions are based on the use of solid colors. If you purchase the pattern and a fabric kit to make this banner, each piece of fabric is labeled with the name of the university and the name of the color. The kit contains solid color fabric. It is much easier to work with solid colors because the right and wrong side of the fabric is often interchangeable. Solid colors also give a crisp clean look to this project.

Another choice is to purchase fabric in the amount indicated on the supplies list in a color that best represents each university color. If you purchase fabric for this project on your own and choose print fabrics, be very careful about pattern placement to be sure the right side of the print is showing on the top side of the banner as sewing progresses. The banner has also been made with tone-on-tone fabrics like batiks, marbles and other textured fabrics. The star point pieces are small and the simpler the fabric, the more effective the design.

The interpretation of each color is deemed accurate by the individual selecting the colors.

Cutting

Be sue to reference the color illustrations (book cover and page 6) to avoid cutting the star point with the wrong orientation, especially if using print fabrics. Some points are left facing and some are right facing. Check and double check!

This is particularly true if using fabrics that have an obvious right side and wrong side. Solid colors can often be flipped if the piece is cut in the wrong orientation.

The little square in the bottom corner of the star point patterns indicate that this is the center seam line for the star point segments.

After deciding whether the right or the left star point pattern piece is needed for each particular color, pin the pattern to each piece of fabric. Be sure the straight grain pattern arrow follows straight grain on fabric.

Use fine silk straight pins because the ruler will be placed over these pins and fine pins lay flatter. Be sure the pins are not sticking out beyond the pattern cutting line. Hitting a pin with the rotary cutter will ruin the cutting blade.

Lay Omnigrid ruler 1/4" (or 1/2" depending upon the side being cut) line along seam line of pattern. Using a rotary cutter, cut along each side of pattern.

Label each star point side with the university name and an arrow to indicate center line of unit. Small sticky labels work well for this step.

Ruler placement and labeling illustrations are shown on page 21.

20

Below is a photo showing the placement of the ruler. Cutting of three sides has already taken place. Of the three already cut sides, one has a 1/2" seam allowance and two have 1/4" wide seam allowances.

Aligned properly, the ruler 1/4" line is on the 1/4" seam line of the pattern. The last side is ready for cutting.

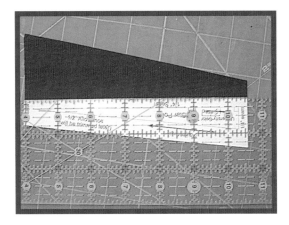

The next photo shows all outside star points cut out and labeled. Each label has the university name and an arrow indicating the center seam line. These are ready for sewing.

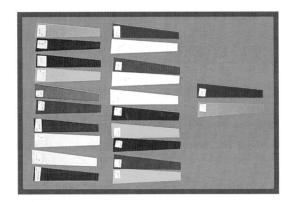

Sewing

Remove school name labels recently added after cutting each set of colors. Remove them just before stitching pairs together. Keep one of the two labels as it will be affixed to the pair after the pair is sewn and pressed. Pin a pair of university star point fabric pieces right sides together along the center line. Center line is indicated by the corner square and the two hatch marks along the pattern center line.

Stitch a 1/4" seam along this line using a short stitch length (about 8-10 stitches per inch). Backstitch at beginning and end. Stitch raw edge to raw edge.

Replace the university name for later reference.

Sew each university color pair together in the same way.

Pressing

Remove label before pressing to avoid leaving a sticky residue on fabric. Press the seam open. Spray each two-color star point with starch. Iron both sides dry and make sure seam is open and flat. Starching helps prevent seams from folding back on themselves. Reattach name label.

Trimming

The following trimming steps are illustrated in the photos on the next page. Numbers correspond to the steps. Use the Star-Point Trimming pattern provided.

1. Cut out the Star-Point Trimming pattern using a rotary cutter. Leave the 1/4" seam allowances attached.

2. Fold the pattern in half lengthwise matching center line at top and bottom to make an accurate fold.

3. Cut a notch out of the center. This is shown in the photo 2-3. This helps align the center seam line of each university color pair accurately before trimming the sewn two-color star point.

4. Lay the trimming pattern on top of the sewn together and pressed two-color star points. Match the pattern center line at top, bottom and middle with the seam line down the center of the fabric pieces.

5. Pin pattern in place. Use fine pins.

6. Place 1/4" line of an Omnigrid ruler along the pattern seam line. Hold ruler securely and trim off excess fabric.

7. Place a fine line of Fray Check on all the raw edges. Let this dry and set these Outside Two-Color Star Points aside for now.

See illustrations on page 22

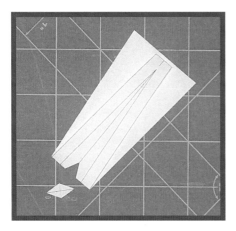

Steps 2.-3. Star Point Trimming pattern folded in half lengthwise with notch cut out of it

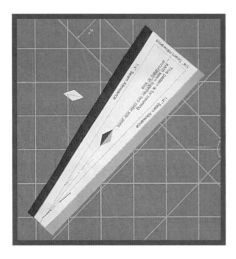

Steps 4-5. Star Point Trimming pattern pinned to sewn star point

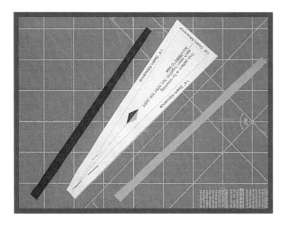

Step 6. Trimmed star point

My University

From east to west
My school's the best.

From north to south
I'll use my mouth,

And let you know there is none better.
Their emblem's stitched upon my sweater.

I see their colors bright and bold.
They are lovely to behold.

My school is a shining star.
I know they're way above the par.

The schooling from my alma mater,
Flowed to me like ink on blotter.

And I learned some impressive words,
For sure, enough to hang with nerds.

Hendecagon is one of many.
It's stuck with me more than any.

My alma mater is the best.
To this again, I will attest.

Beatrice Hughes

Construction

Folded Inside Triangular Star Points

Fabric Requirements

Each Triangular star point pattern requires a piece of fabric 3-1/2" wide and 3" high (straight grain). Use the darker of the two university colors for this piece. For example Iowa colors are black and gold. Use the black for this pattern piece. You will have plenty of fabric in the 1/4" yard purchased to accommodate this pattern piece.

Cutting

Cut eleven units from the Inside Triangular Star Point pattern. Cut one for each of the DARKER of the two university colors.

Making the Triangles

1. Fold wrong sides together along the length, bringing the hatch marks together and press flat.

2. Fold right (**R**) side to back of center. Press flat.

3. Fold left (**L**) side to back of center. Press flat. This results in a triangular unit.

4. The fabric triangle will have wings at the top raw edge that cross each other. This keeps the fabric folds on the back from showing at the folded edges and eliminates some bulk.

5. Cut out and use the Inside Triangular Star Point Pattern Checker (on the Checker and Trimmer Page) to check for size accuracy of the folded fabric triangles. Make any necessary folding adjustments. Trim the wings above the raw edge off even with the top of the pattern.

6. Stitching by hand, use about 3-4 whipstitches in the same place to secure layers together at the center hatch mark. Be sure to keep the whipstitch small so it will not show in later sewing steps. When whipstitching, pass the needle through the loop of thread that forms to knot off. Knot off in the same manner a couple times and then cut the thread leaving a small tail.

Set the Inside Triangular Star Points aside for now.

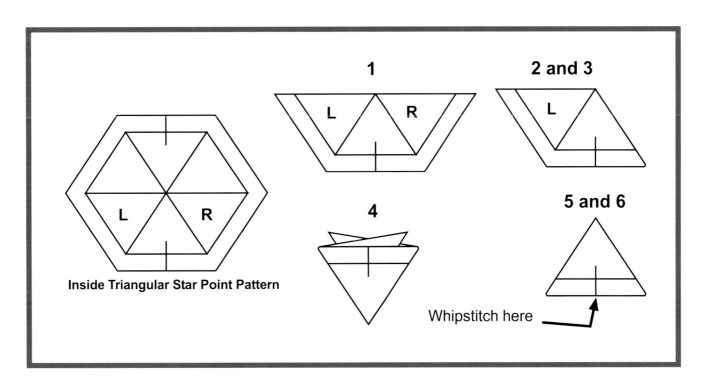

Inside Triangular Star Point Pattern

Whipstitch here

Organization Logo Unit

Supplies Needed

A picture or electronic copy of the organization's logo is needed for transferring the logo to the fabric printer sheet.

An inkjet printer fabric sheet is the material to which the logo is transferred. The fabric sheet is described in the list of supplies on page 2. There is a printer fabric sheet included in the fabric kit. Both brands listed remain soft and flexible after printing and soaking.

Some copy centers can print logos on fabric. Check your local stores for this service should you not have the equipment needed to print on the fabric sheet.

Another approach is to embroider the logo on a piece of white fabric which is larger than needed for the center hendecagon. An embroidery sewing machine could be used or it can be done by hand. After embroidering, cut the fabric to size using the pattern supplied.

Whether printing from the computer, using a copy center service or using embroidery, assess the logo size. It should fit attractively in the center of the hendecagon pattern. Page 12 shows an example of how the MSUCC logo fits.

When printing from your computer equipment, a scanner to scan the image or a disc with a digital copy of the logo is needed to print using an ink jet printer.

Finally, an ink jet printer is needed.

Process

Scan or open a good copy of the organization's logo into a suitable software application. Measure the Inside Hendecagon pattern and scale the logo to fit inside the pattern piece. Be sure to allow for the Inside Triangular Star Points.

The same approach is used if using a digital image file from a disc. Open the file and transfer the logo to a program from which you can print onto the printer fabric sheet.

As shown in the schematic with the pattern on page 12, two Organizational Logo Units can be cut from one sheet of printer fabric. Arrange logo in software application so that if a mistake is made, the sheet can be turned end to end and printed a second time.

Test your logo size and spacing by printing the logo on an 8-1/2" x 11" piece of paper. Then test the logo under the pattern on an illuminated light table. Make logo size adjustments before printing it to the fabric printer sheet.

After making adjustments, print the logo on the fabric printer sheet according to the manufacturer's directions. The directions come with the sheets and are included in the kit.

Aligning the Logo

After the logo has been printed on the printer using the fabric sheet, follow the manufacturer's directions and carefully remove the paper backing. Then treat and dry the fabric according to those directions. Carefully iron the logo area.

Follow the directions below for pattern placement and fabric cutting.

1. Lay the Organization Logo pattern right side down on an illuminated light table. It does not matter if the pattern is right side up or down but it is best to lay it printed side down. It helps eliminate the possibility of transferring the ink of the printed pattern lines onto the fabric containing the logo.

Tape the Organization Logo pattern securely to the illuminated light table. The MSU letters should be at the top. That is the reference for orienting the top of the logo. The bottom of the logo should be parallel to the top line on the hendecagon pattern.

2. Place the printed fabric containing the organization's logo right side down over the Organization Logo pattern. Center the logo inside the triangular points. Use the cross hairs in the center of the pattern to help in alignment. The MSU letters should be at the top. After checking and being satisfied with the position of the logo, tape the fabric in place over the pattern.

3. Use a straight edge and a fine point water soluble blue pen and trace the outline of the Organizational Logo pattern along all the cutting lines. Be sure that the lines cross as they do on the pattern.

4. Trace the seam lines in the same way. The seam lines are where the Outside Two-Color Star Point Units will be aligned and sewn to the Inside Triangular Star Points and Logo Unit.

5. Place a blue water soluble dot at each Inside Triangular Star Point shown on the Center Hendecagon pattern. These dots are for aligning the colored fabric Inside Triangular Star Points.

Cutting

Cut out the Organizational Logo center unit. Use an Omnigrid ruler and rotary cutter to cut along the cutting lines of the Organizational Logo drawn on the back of the printer fabric. Be sure to place the 1/4" line of the ruler along the seam line to help insure accuracy of cut.

Place a fine line of Fray Check on the raw edges and let it dry. It dries quickly and can be ironed dry but first cover it with a pressing cloth.

Changes You May Want to Make

The pattern is designed to distribute the university colors evenly, in particular, the white, cream and yellow colors. The MSU colors are shown at the top of the design but your alma mater Outside Two-Color Star Point and Inside Triangular Star Point can be rotated to the top even though the MSU outside star point colors are shown at top of this design.

Changing the location of your university Outside Two-Color Star Point location will influence where your Inside Triangular Star Point's color is placed. The corresponding Outside Two-Color Star Points and Inside Triangular Star Points need to coordinate with each other. Rotate your Inside Triangular Star Point adjacent to your Outside Two-Color Star Point colors.

Keeping the colors distributed as in the original design, page 26 illustrates eleven rotations. Look for your school colors at the top and see if the color distribution is pleasing to you.

Finally, when choosing color layout, arrange both the outside and inside star point colors to suit you. This is your prerogative.

If the decision to rotate or rearrange the colors is made, keep these changes in mind as you proceed through the following steps.

Placing the Inside Triangular Star Points

Each Inside Triangular Star Point has already been prepared. Refer to the color illustrated banner on page 6 for placement of Inside Triangular Star Point colors.

If you rotated your school colors to the top of the design, all the remaining Inside Triangular Star Points will also be rotated in the same direction. Match the Outside Two-Color Star Point university colors and the Inside Triangular Star Point colors accurately.

If the colors were completely rearranged, also take this into account. Then follow the steps below.

1. Use the water soluble glue stick and, on the right side of the Organization Logo Unit and with the MSU at the top, place a fine line of glue between the cutting line and seam line. The glue is to adhere each Inside Triangular Star Point to the Logo Unit temporarily.

As you proceed through successive steps, adhere one Triangular Star Point at a time.

2. Match the tip of the folded Inside Triangular Star Point to the dot on the Logo Unit. The dot is on the wrong side of the Logo Unit. Doing this step on an illuminated light table will help in alignment.

Finger-press the raw edge of the Inside Triangular Star Point to the glue on the Logo Unit. Check alignment and check that the raw edges are even. Pin in place. Let the glue dry.

3. Continue gluing, aligning, finger-pressing and pinning each Inside Triangular Star Point. Be sure to check that color placement is correct.

4. Once all star points are arranged, turn the unit to the back and machine stitch just outside (toward the cutting line) the seam line that was drawn on the back of the Logo Unit.

The Center Logo Unit combined with the Inside Triangular Star Points is now ready to sew to the larger Outside Two-Color Star Point and A-B-C Unit.

Set this Logo and Inside Triangular Star Point Unit aside for now. The A-B-C Units and Outside Two-Color Star Point Units will be sewn together next.

Color Distribution with Your School Colors at the Top

Each permutation shows how the balance of colors changes.

Locate your school colors at the top to decide if you like the new color balance.

Combining the A-B-C Wing Units
and the
Outside Two-Color Star Points

The marking steps that follow are important for alignment and should not be skipped.

Marking A-B-C Unit Alignment Dots

Use the A-B-C Pattern Trimmer to help in placement of alignment dots.

1. Cut off the top of the pattern between points QQ, which reduces the size of the pattern. Be sure to leave the pattern line visible.

2. Create an alignment window by cutting a triangular shape out at the base of part C of the pattern where the letter Y would be. This window helps align the stitching lines with the pattern lines.

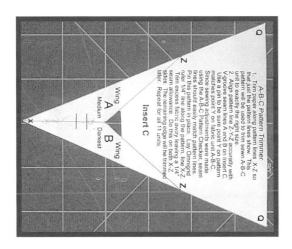

Steps 1 and 2
Trimming the A-B-C Pattern

3. Turn the sewn A-B-C fabric unit to the wrong side. Place the A-B-C Pattern Trimmer on the back of the sewn unit. Align the pattern window opening with the V-grove of the A-B-C fabric unit. Also align the bottom pattern point with the A-B seam line. Pin in place. Use a water soluble blue pen or a white pencil and place a dot at the top edge at each Q side. These dots are to align the top of the Outside

Two-Color Star Point unit. They should be 1/4" from the edge of X-Q side.

4. Place a dot at the base of the pattern at X. This should be 1/4" from the base of the sewn unit. This is for aligning the bottom of the Outside Two-Color Star Point unit.

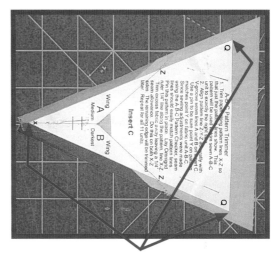

Steps 3 and 4
Place a dot along the base at each Q point and at the point by X

Mark all eleven units in the same way.

The next step is to place alignment dots on the star points.

Marking the Outside Two-Color Star Point Units

Use a ruler for these steps. Mark on the wrong side of units. During successive steps, these marks are for accurately pinning at corresponding points on the A-B-C Units.

1. Place a mark 1/4" from the raw edge at bottom corners of the unit. The two marks will also be 1/4" from the side raw edges.

2. Place a Line at the top of the Outside Two-Color Star Point Unit 1/4" from the top raw edge.

Place the marks on all eleven units. Marking locations for one unit are pointed out by the red arrows below.

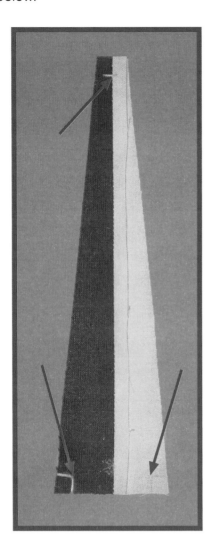

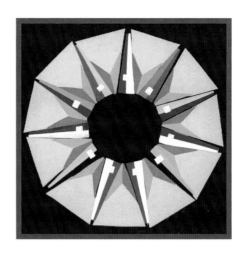

Preparation

Arrange all the Outside Two-Color Star Points and the A-B-C Units in the illustrated color order. Right side is up.

If placing your university colors at the top of the design, rotate the unit until those colors are at the top of the design.

Check to be sure the school colors are in the desired orientation.

The next photo shows the Outside Two-Color Star Points and the A-B-C Units arranged before the pinning and sewing processes begin.

Pinning

Pin through left side dots at top and bottom of star points into the corresponding alignment dots on the left side of the A-B-C Unit. Carefully match dots. Pin along entire edge and be sure raw edges align. Pin one Star Point Unit to one A-B-C Wing section. Remove star point labels so you do not sew them into the seam and save labels. Replace labels after sewing is complete.

Pin all eleven star points together before beginning to sew. Below is a picture of the Outside Two-Color Star Points pinned to the A-B-C Wing Units.

Sewing

Sew from dot to dot and not from raw edge to raw edge. Sew on Outside Two-Color Star Point side so it is easy to see where to start and stop stitching.

Begin by sewing from the wide edge of star point and sew to the narrow end. Take a 1/4" seam allowance. Back stitch at each dot.

When all eleven segments are sewn, each new segment will contain an A-B-C Unit and an Outside Two-Color Star Point.

After sewing all eleven star points to the left side of an A-B-C Wing Unit, the next step is joining two of the units just sewn. Pin, matching alignment dots. Also carefully match and pin raw edges.

This time the sewing begins at the narrow end of the star point and goes to the wide end of the star point. This allows the alignment dots to be seen while sewing. Back stitch at the beginning and end of each alignment dot.

Continue sewing pairs together. Then join larger units in the same way until all eleven Outside Two-Color Star Points and A-B-C Units are together.

Pressing is the next step.

Pressing

The photos below show three stages of pressing.

1. Press star points open away from the center star point seam allowance. They are pressed toward Insert C.

The seams at the center of the unit by the wide end of the star point overlap each other so it is easiest to begin by pressing one star point seam allowance as described above.

Then skip one and press the next. Work around the unit toward where pressing began. Because there are eleven points, there will be two un-pressed points as you reach the point where you began pressing. Photo 1 below shows the unpressed areas.

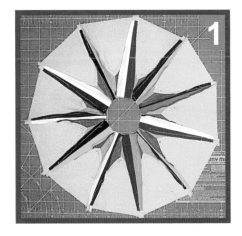

Above, the green and white and
the red and white points are pressed but
the two between are not yet pressed.

2. Skip one and press the next star point toward the first star point that was pressed. The wide end of the star point will overlap the first one pressed. Smooth and flatten the fabrics where they overlap.

Continue working around the unit pressing in the same way until all the star points are pressed open and all overlap smoothly at the wide end. Photo 2 shows the wrong side of the pressed unit.

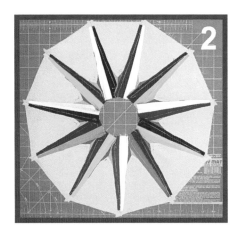

3. When this pressing is complete, turn the unit to the right side and press the front so that all seams lay flat and smooth. Photo 3 shows the right side of the unit with all seams pressed.

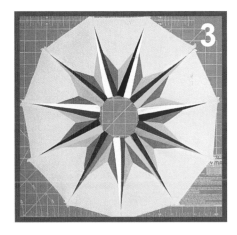

Pay attention to pressing direction because it will make sewing easier later.

The A-B-C Unit combined with the Outside Two-Color Star Point Unit is complete and ready for the center Inside Triangular Star Point Unit.

Combining

Outside Two-Color Star Point and A-B-C Wing Unit
Joined to
Inside Triangular Star Point and Organization Logo Unit

Alignment Points

Pairs of Alignment Points:

Pair One: These are the points marked on the wide end of the Outside Two-Color Star Points. They are to the left and right of the center seam line and are the points where stitching stopped when joining the Outside Two-Color Star Points to the A-B-C Unit.

Pair Two: These are where the seam line marked on the backside of the logo unit cross. They are to the left and right of each Inside Triangular Star Point. These crossing points become the matching points that align with the stopping points at the wide end of the Outside Two-Color Star Points edges.

Matching and Pinning

Begin with the MSU Outside Two-Color Star Point wide edge and the MSU Inside Triangular Star Point. Place the Inside Triangular Star Point and Logo Unit right side up on the worktable. Place the MSU Outside Two-Color Star Point and A-B-C Unit wrong side up on top of the Inside Triangular Star Point and Logo Unit. Photo 1 below shows these areas.

Match the seam line crossing points on the backside of the Inside Triangular Star Point and Logo Unit to the stopping points at the wide end of the Outside Two-Color Star Point wrong side.

Pin through the right stopping point on the Outside Two-Color Star Point (white side of two-color star point) through to the crossing point on the logo wrong side seam line at the right of the MSU Inside Triangular Star Point. In the same way, then pin the left side.

Photo 2 shows the first two matched points and the first two pins in place. Pins show near the raw edge at the top seam line.

Instead of pinning, you can Tie Tack these points. It is easier and more accurate than joining with pins. It is typically also less time-consuming. See page 52 for directions. This method helps ensure accurate matching.

Photo 3, on page 31, shows another view of pinning but this photo is of the Logo Unit backside with a portion of the pins showing at the seam line.

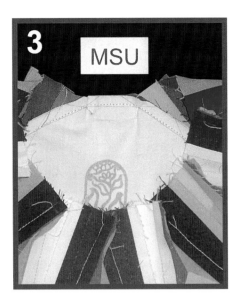

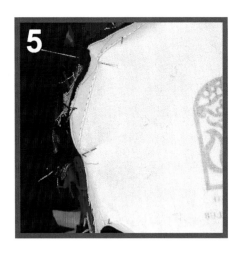

Continue to match points and pin (or Tie Tack), working around the two units. Photo 4 shows the matching points of both units pinned together with additional pins along the hendecagon edges to align the raw edges of both units.

If using Tie Tacking, there only needs to be pins along the hendecagon sides to keep the raw edges even on both units.

Sewing

Stitch these two units together using a neutral thread and stitch on the seam line marked on the Logo Unit back. Stitch all the way around the unit. Flatten and straighten the fabric on the bottom as sewing progresses and be sure the bottom seams lay in the direction pressed.

At seam line crossing points, always be sure sewing machine needle is in the fabric layers and then lift the presser foot at each crossing point. Turn the fabric, arrange and smooth out wrinkles in the fabric underneath, lower foot and continue sewing. Over-stitch at the end. This means to stitch beyond the beginning stitching point.

Sewing the Inside Triangular Star Point and Logo Unit to the Outside Two-Color Star Point and A-B-C Unit is complete. Turn the completed combined units to the right side. The Inside Triangular Star Points will stick straight up.

Photo 6 below shows the Inside Triangular Star Points sticking straight up.

Photo 5, at the right, is a close-up view. The stitching, added after joining the Inside Triangular Star Points to the Logo Unit, is showing on the logo backside.

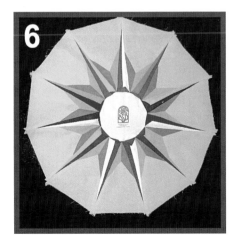

The next step is pressing the points flat.

Pressing

Lay the Inside-Outside Star Point-Logo stitched unit on an ironing surface right side up. Spritz the entire unit with water to relax the fabrics. Also, turn the unit over and spritz the back with water. Gently tug on a Inside Triangular Star Point and finger press each point flat in the direction of the logo. On the back side, finger-press the seams toward the Outside Two-Color Star Point.

Finger press means to rub your finger along the seam using some pressure to encourage the seam to lay in the desired direction.

Spritz with water again to relax fabric then iron with steam iron until all Inside Triangular Star Points lay flat.

Turn the unit right side down and press the back of the unit with a steam iron.

The Inside and Outside Star Point Unit is pressed and ready for the next step. Photo 7 shows the pressed units.

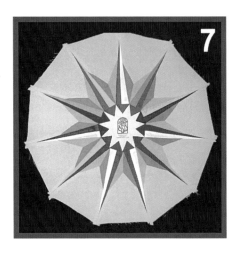

The next step is making the seam line around the C sections of the unit.

Marking the Outside Seam Line

Trim the seam allowance off the A-B-C Pattern Checker. The part that remains is the Insert C part of the pattern. Photo 8 shows the A-B-C Pattern Checker trimmed.

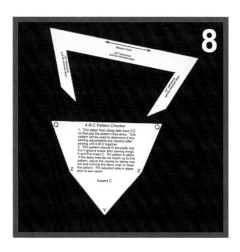

Place the A-B-C Pattern Checker on front of the combined and pressed star unit as shown in the Photo 9 below.

The area of the pattern checker that will fit the best is point Y. Pin pattern in place at Y. Because of the seams, the match at each side of QZ will need to be averaged. Center the pattern. Pin it in place at QQ. The QQ side should line up with the star points. Adjust as necessary.

Place a straight edge between QQ and align with top edge of pattern. Use the fine point blue water soluble pen and mark each of the eleven sides. This is the seam line for sewing the background to the star unit. The seam area will be greater than 1/4". Do not trim this now. It will be trimmed after the background is stitched to the star unit.

After marking the seam lines, the unit is ready to have the background attached. Set this central unit aside for now.

Using the Hendecagon Page

Making the Pattern for Marking and Cutting the Background Fabric

The pattern is relatively easy to make. Page 13 contains an illustration of the Hendecagon Page however, use the pattern included with all patterns, which begin on page 61. That pattern contains important red lines, which facilitate its use. Do not copy the Hendecagon Page because there is a chance the copy will not be at 100% which would alter the pattern size, making the outcome undesirable. Follow the directions below.

1. Cut a sheet of plain paper that is 26" x 30" (craft or other drawing paper). This is larger than the finished size of the banner. See illustration below.

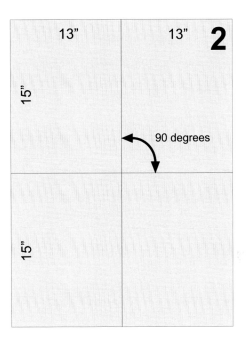

Hendecagon Page with the horizontal and vertical centers of the 26" x 30" page. Check alignment then tape the Hendecagon Page down securely. Masking or 3-M Scotch tape work well. See illustration below.

2. Draw horizontal and vertical lines through the center of the paper. Half of 26" is 13". Half of 30" is 15". Be sure they are at 90 degree angles. See first illustration at the right.

3. Place the center of the Hendecagon Page on the center of the 26" x 30" paper. The white area with the red lines is the Hendecagon Page.

Line up the horizontal dashed line and the vertical dashed lines at the top and bottom of the

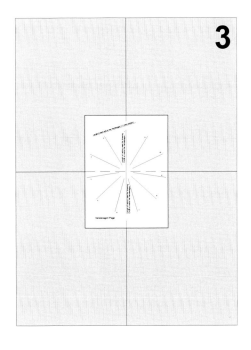

4. Use a yardstick compass to draw the large circle necessary to make the right size hendecagon. Griffin makes the compass points sold by Blick Art Supplies. Their web is: www.dickblick.com/zz554/33/. The compass points are also available in some catalogs, quilting, craft and art supply stores. A picture of the compass points follows. You will also need a yardstick or long straight piece of wood that fits the opening in each compass point, which houses the yardstick.

The black line down the center of the Hendecagon Page is the radius of the circle used to make the Hendecagon. The distance between the point of the compass and the lead end of the compass needs to exactly match the length of the black line down the center of the page. Adjust the compass points to fit the radius line.

5. Place the metal point of the compass on the exact center of the Hendecagon Page where the horizontal and vertical lines cross. Accurately draw the circle on the 26" x 30" paper. The drawn circle is shown in the illustration below.

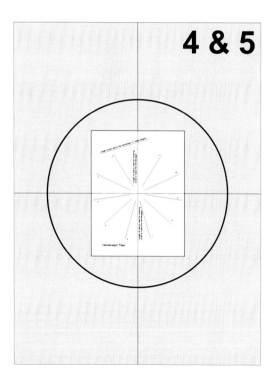

6. Lay a ruler down the length of the line numbered 1 (the black line which was also used to set the distance between the compass points). Accurately draw out from the horizontal center to just past the

edge of the circle. Repeat this process on the red lines numbered 2 through 11. The lines do not need to begin at the center but use the center point to help align the ruler before drawing each radiating line. The next illustration shows the drawn lines.

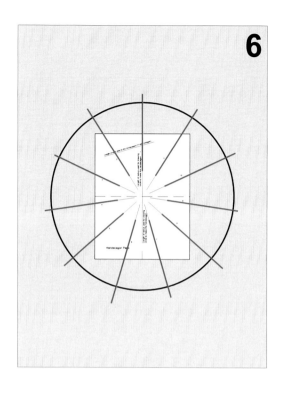

7. After finishing each radiating line, lay a ruler between lines 1 and 2 where they touch the large circle drawn in step 5. This is shown in the next illustration.

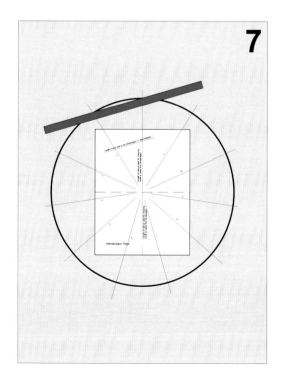

8. Draw a line between those two points. Repeat this drawing process for all eleven sides of the hendecagon.

Each side length should match the length of the line at the top of the Hendecagon Page. The completed hendecagon will look like the one in the next illustration.

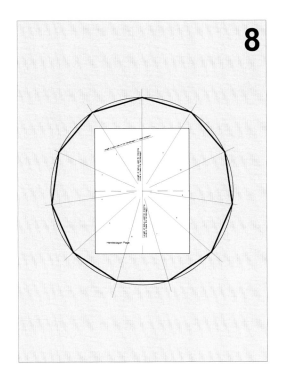

9. Lay the 1/4" line of an Omnigrid ruler along each of the 11 sides and draw exactly 1/4" <u>inside</u> the large hendecagon just completed.

This process is a seam allowance adjustment.

The smaller hendecagon just drawn will be the part of the pattern utilized in the next phase of banner construction.

The following illustration shows the smaller hendecagon inside the first larger hendecagon.

There is one other simple step for completing the pattern.

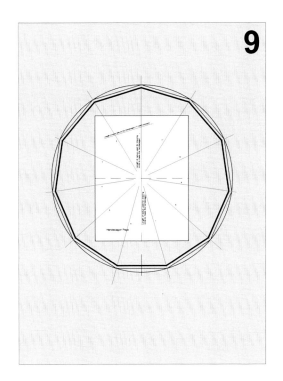

10. Place a #1 at the top MSU line. Place a #6 and #7 at the bottom two lines.

Place a tick mark between 6 and 7 to indicate the center point between 6 and 7.

After adding the lines, drawing each hendecagon, adding the numbers and placing the tick mark, the illustration below is what it will look like. The pattern is complete. Using this pattern to cut the background is the next phase.

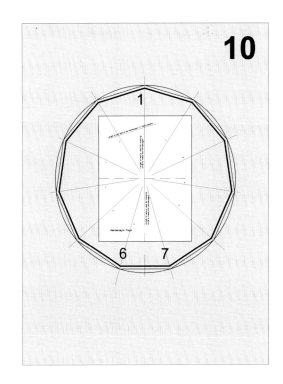

Using the Hendecagon Pattern

You have just made the pattern for the background. Next is a series of steps for cutting the background fabric using the pattern just made.

Cutting the Background Fabric

1. The center of the hendecagon pattern is the part used in the steps that follow. Rotary cut the center out of the pattern along the <u>smaller</u> hendecagon line. Be sure the line itself is still visible. Set this pattern aside for the moment.

2. Cut a piece of background fabric 22" wide by 34" long. The 34" length is cut on the straight grain of the fabric. Note: it is desirable to have 44" wide fabric. See the alternate background cutting layout on page 9 if the fabric is not 44" wide. Adjust the cutting according to the width of the background fabric.

3. Using a fine point blue water soluble pen by Mark-B-Gone, and on the fabric <u>right side</u>, mark a dot at the center of the top and bottom of this background piece. For example, half of 22" is 11". Draw a fine line between the two center dots down the length. This line is shown in the next illustration.

4. Place a dot 5" down from the top raw edge of the backing fabric on the blue centerline. The fabric setup will look similar to the drawing below but dots on drawing are exaggerated.

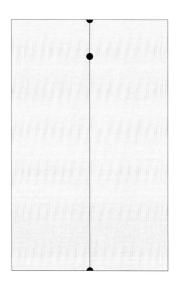

5. At the dot that is 5" down, align the top of the Hendecagon pattern cutout. The top is where the number one is printed. A picture of the pattern placement is below. Pin pattern in place on the background fabric at number 1.

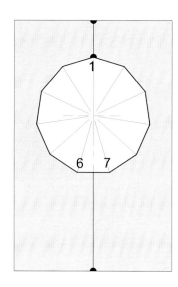

6. Place the center hatch mark between 6 and 7 points on the center line of the fabric and pin in place.

7. Place additional pins around the Hendecagon pattern so it lays flat and is securely attached to the background fabric.

8. Lay the 1/4" line of an Omnigrid ruler on the pattern cutting line; and with the fine point blue water soluble pen, draw around the pattern. Be sure these lines cross slightly because the crossing points will be used as matching points. Mark all around the pattern. The seam line is being marked.

Page 37 shows two photos of this process. The first shows the ruler 1/4" line along the edge of the pattern so that the 1/4" line along the ruler is outside the pattern edge.

The second photo shows a close up of this process. Look carefully and you will see that the first blue line has been drawn. Note that the dots on the ruler along the 1/4" line are on the edge of the pattern. Accurate alignment is important.

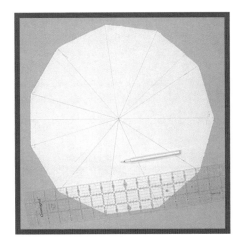

Marking is in Progress

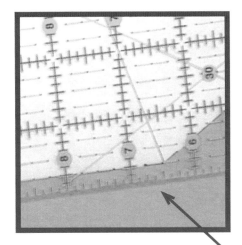

Close up of Ruler and First Marking
The next side is ready to be marked.

The blue line from previously
marked side is showing here.

9. Remove the pattern.

10. Lay the Omnigrid 1/4" line along the seam line just marked. Mark 1/4" <u>inside</u> the marked seam line. These lines are the cutting line.

11. Carefully cut out the center of the fabric on the cutting line. Either use a rotary cutter and ruler or scissors.

12. Place a pin dot of Fray Check at each crossing point on the drawn hendecagon seam line. Let it dry.

Next is a photo of the background with the center cut out. It is laying on a black surface.

13. Clip from the raw edge of the hendecagon diagonally to the crossing points of the drawn hendecagon seam line (to where the dot of Fray Check was added). Do not clip beyond the drawn seam line.

14. Fray Check the clipped raw edges. Fray check along the remaining raw edges of the hendecagon.

Sewing

1. Fold along the drawn seam line and fold it to the wrong side of the background. Pin in place. Repeat this all around the background unit.

2. Lay the combined A-B-C and Outside Two-Color Star Point Unit and Inside Triangular Star Point and Logo Unit right side up on the worktable. If your university color is to be rotated to the top, rotate it now. Lay the background unit right side up on top of the combined star unit.

Align the edges of the background which have been folded under with the seam lines marked on the combined star point units. The 5" part of the background is the top of the background. In the previous illustrations, that 5" is above the MSU star point.

3. Match the points of the outside star with the crossing points on the background. Pin the background to Star Point Unit. Tie tack the points to ensure accuracy of matching. See page 52, which illustrates how to Tie Tack.

4. Stitch along the seam lines using an invisible stitch. The banner top is now sewn together.

Pressing

1. Lay the banner right side up on a terry cloth towel on top of an ironing surface.

2. Spritz the area just sewn. Some of the blue marks may disappear but may come back when pressing. Later the entire banner will be immersed in water and all blue line will disappear.

3. Be sure the iron is at a medium heat to prevent scorching. Press the unit on the right side. Press it dry.

4. Cover the center of the banner with a cloth. The background cutout can be used to cover the area. Spray starch the background and press dry. Lay banner top back on worktable.

The banner is now ready for squaring.

Eleven More Fun Facts

1. Throughout Europe, a 1999 a total solar eclipse happened on August 11 at 11:11 a.m.
2. The number 11 can be read upside down or right side up and it stays the same. It is the fourth number to have that characteristic. Others are 0, 1 and 8.
3. The bottom of the Mariana Trench, at 11km, is the deepest point of the ocean floor.
4. The stylized maple leaf on the Canadian flag has 11 points.
5. The Number 11 Bus is a low-cost way of sightseeing in London.
6. At 11 feet long, the Siberian tiger is the largest cat.
7. In English, 11 is the smallest positive integer requiring three syllables.
8. In a year, day 254 is September 11 and 2 + 5 + 4 = 11.
9. November is month 11.
10. The total number of characters in Jesus Christ is 11.
11. It is recorded that Jesus appeared 11 times after his death upon the cross.

Squaring Banner

Squaring the banner is the final step before adding the batting and backing.

Marking

Directions below talk about measuring from specific university color sets. If your university colors were rotated to the top, substitute the new color orientation for those in the directions below.

1. Measure from the Wisconsin star point to the raw edge of the background side. Write that figure down and label it for future reference.

2. Measure from the Indiana star point to the raw edge on the background side. Write that figure down and label that number. It will also be referenced.

3. Select the smallest of the two measurements. Place a straight edge between the Wisconsin and Indiana points and place a dot at the edge of the background on each side representing the smaller of the two distances from each star point toward the background side raw edge.

4. Measure between the two dots. That is the width used to square the banner sides. Write that figure down and label it. Divide that measurement in half. For example in the photo below, the measurement between the dot to the left of Indiana and to the right of Wisconsin is 20-3/4". Half of that is 10-3/8".

The small measure in the photo shows the distance from the Indiana star point to the banner raw edge.

5. Measure the top and bottom background widths. This step is part of squaring process. The two measurements will likely be different. Divide each width in half. It is helpful to write these measurements down.

6. Find the top and bottom center marks placed when using the hendecagon pattern. At the top and bottom background center marks, place a dot to the left and right of center half the Indiana-Wisconsin measurement found in step 4.

This Wisconsin-Indiana measurement should be smaller than either the top or the bottom measurements taken in step 5. If there is a difference, measure the top, bottom and center again. Use the smallest distance.

Squaring Sides

Be sure the banner is laying flat on the cutting surface.

1. Lay a straight edge the length of the banner along the three dots just made (one at top, one by the star point and one at the bottom). Test both sides before cutting to be sure all marks are in alignment. See the photo below. The first banner side is ready to be trimmed along the right side of the banner.

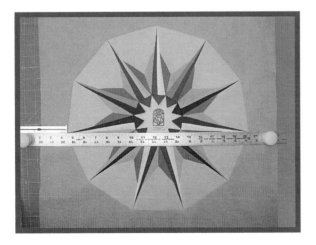

2. Have someone help hold the straight edge to prevent it from moving. Clamping the ruler to the table edge and taping it securely, as shown in the previous photo, is another way of keeping the ruler from moving. Use a rotary cutter and cut along the straight edge.

Do this on each long side.

3. Run a fine line of Fray Check down both sides and let it dry.

Squaring Top

The banner is longer than it will be after being squared. The top of the background is the area that needs to be trimmed first. Then the bottom is trimmed. Use the lines on the rotary cutting mat to square up the banner top and bottom.

1. Lay the banner on the matt and move it until a line on the mat is just slightly covered by the banner top edge. The banner sides should lay squarely against the matt guide lines.

3. Have someone help hold the straight edge. Use a rotary cutter and trim off the banner top uneven edge. This is shown in the photo below.

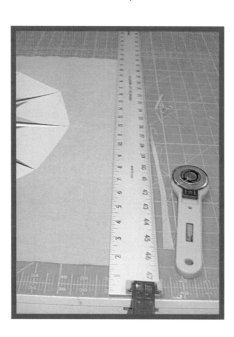

Squaring Bottom

Cut longer than needed, the banner background is now cut to the proper length and squared.

1. Accurately measure 28-1/2" down from the top. Place a dot at each side of the background.

2. Place a ruler along the dots just marked. Trim off the excess at the bottom. The next photo shows that the bottom is in the process of being trimmed

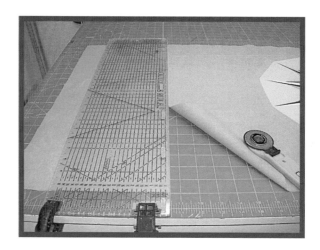

3. Run a fine line of Fray Check along the top and bottom raw edges. Let it dry.

Trimming the Inside-Outside Star Point Unit Seam Line

The seam allowance on the Inside-Outside Star Point-Logo Unit was left untrimmed after the background was sewn to it. Now it is time to trim the seam allowance to 1/4". Steps to trim this follow.

1. As shown in the photo below, fold the just squared background fabric that was sewn to the star unit out of the way so the QQ seam line is visible.

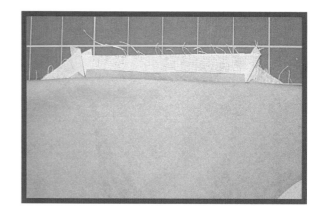

2. Lay the 1/4" line of an Omnigrid ruler along the seam line. Be sure to align the 1/4" line of dots on the ruler along the stitching line of the star and logo where it attached to the background. See photo on page 41.

40

3. Use a rotary cutter and trim off the excess fabric from the QQ edge of Insert C.

The next two photos show the ruler alignment and the trimming steps. Repeat these steps on the rest of the QQ sides.

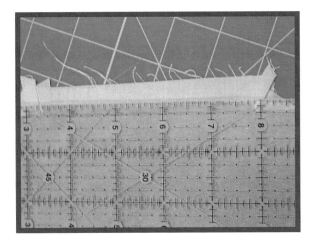

Ruler Alignment

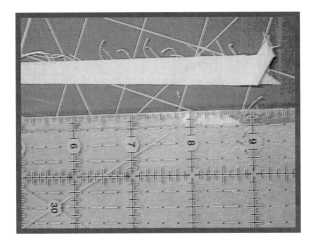

Excess Fabric Trimmed

The banner top is now complete and ready to be marked for quilting and then to have the batting and backing added.

Take some time to pat yourself on the back for achieving a completed top. Congratulations!

The next photo shows the completed banner top pinned to a design wall.

Marking Quilting Design

Below are steps to mark the suggested quilting design for a 20" x 28" banner (finished size). Steps about how to develop the design are below. Each step is illustrated. The illustrations appear in sequence of the steps and are on pages 44 and 45.

Do all marking with a blue water soluble pen. These marks will be washed out when quilting is complete.

The word "about" is used because every banner will have slightly different measurements so an approximation is given.

Dots in the illustrations are exaggerated to bring attention to their location and for improved visibility.

Outside the Center Logo

See Figures 1 through 11 (pages 44 and 45) that illustrate the following steps.

1. Draw lines between the Wing Points A and B across Insert C. These lines should be parallel to the edge of the hendecagon seam line that joins it to the background, about 2" to 2-1/8" from the seam line. Before drawing the line, check the measurement around the unit and select one that fits best.

2. Find the center of each side of the hendecagon and place a dot there. Pass the line through the dot just positioned, drawing the line from the V-groove between Wings A and B to the outer raw edge of the banner.

Note the alpha designations at the outer edge of each radiating line. They indicate pairs of lines that are equidistant from the sides and/or top and bottom of the banner raw edges. Measure each pair and make adjustments so the pair measurements are alike. Use these lines for lining up other design lines in the steps that follow. The letter **F** runs down the middle of the banner bottom and should be at the center of the banner bottom.

3. Place a dot 1-1/2" from the hendecagon seam line on each of the radiating lines. Connect the dots to make a rotated hendecagon. This connection is shown by the dashed red line.

4. On the newly drawn hendecagon, find the center of each side between the radiating lines. Place a dot at that center. Using a straight edge placed down the center of the Outside Two-Color Star Points, pass the ruler through the dots. Draw a line from the star point out to the banner raw edge. This is shown by the radiating blue dashed line. Measure out 1" from the edge of the hendecagon dot and place a new dot on the line just drawn. This is shown by the blue dot in the illustration. Repeat the dots around the unit.

Use a ruler and draw from each of those blue dots on the blue dashed line to where the red dashed line crosses the first hendecagon drawn. Repeat this process around the unit. When connected, the line make a shallow pointed star.

5. Measure from the bottom raw edge up the center line **F** 1" and place a dot there. Draw lines from that dot to the points of Wings A and B. Measure the distance from the dot to the line that crosses Insert C between the points of Wings A and B. Write that figure down and label it. The measurement will be about 10-1/2" long.

On **E** lines, measure from the seam at insert C the distance found above (about 10-1/2"). Place a dot on the line. Connect the points as shown in the illustrations. There will be three star points all the same length.

6. At the top of the banner measure down 1" from the raw edge and place a dot on **A** lines. Draw lines from that dot to the Wing Points A and B. Measure the distance from the point to the line that crosses Insert C. Write that figure down and label it.

On **B** lines, measure the distance found above up from the line that crosses Insert C and place a dot on the line. This distance is shown by the two dots on the left **B** line. Connect the dot to the Wing Points A and B to create four star points all the same size.

7. At **C** and **D** lines, connect Wings A and B points to the center of the rotated hendecagon side. The four same-size star points will not extend past the hendecagon but will be inside the rotated hendecagon.

8. Go to Step 4 and find the dot that refers to the center of the first hendecagon line. Measure up (down at the bottom of the banner) 3" and place a dot on, what, in the illustration, is a blue dashed line. Place a dot on the line. Repeat this process on the remaining sides.

Connect the dots as shown. Seven arrowhead shapes will result, three at the top and four at the bottom. These are shown by the black dashed lines in the illustration 8.

9. On the lines that extend from the star points between **E** and **F**, measure down 7" from the Outside Two-Color Star Point. Place a dot at that point. Do this on both sides of center.

10. On the lines that extend from the top star points between **A** and **B**, measure up 6" from the Outside Two-Color Star Point.

11. Connect the remaining lines as illustrated, and shown in black, to help identify them.

The green circles on the large illustration are a potential location for the university pins. Another potential site is on each Inside Triangular Star Point.

Inside Center Logo Hendecagon

Quilting will be around the outside edges of the logo and in other areas of the logo to enhance the design. It may not be necessary to mark these lines if the outline of the logo is linear. If not, mark the lines for quilting reference. Mark 1/2" from the edge of the central hendecagon that contains the logo. This will be under the Inside Triangular Star Points. See the quilting pattern below.

If no logo is used, draw around the outside edge of the Inside Triangular Star Points. This will be one quilting area. The line will be at the edge of the Triangular Star Points.

Then, find the center of the hendecagon and draw lines between each triangular star point to the center. This is shown below.

How to Use the Full Size Center Hendecagon Quilting Pattern

1. Cut the pattern out on outside edges. Use the pattern at the end of the book.
2. Center paper pattern in center of logo hendecagon.
3. Rotate the pattern so that the points of the hendecagon are under the star points.
4. Pin the pattern in place when satisfied with location.
5. Draw around pattern edges with water soluble blue pen.
6. Quilt on drawn lines.

Tip: Pin the Inside Triangular Star Points out of the way to aid in marking and then quilting.

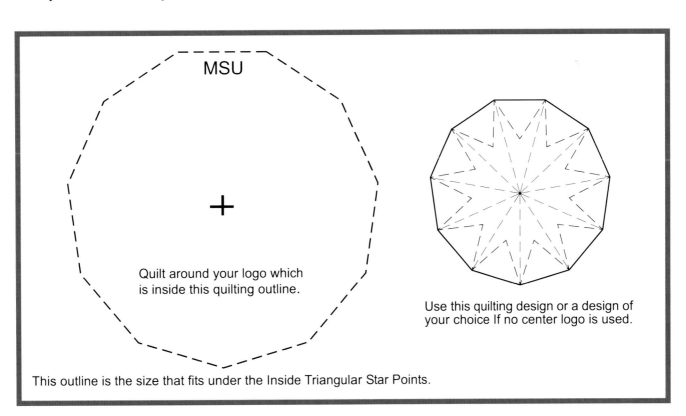

MSU

+

Quilt around your logo which is inside this quilting outline.

Use this quilting design or a design of your choice If no center logo is used.

This outline is the size that fits under the Inside Triangular Star Points.

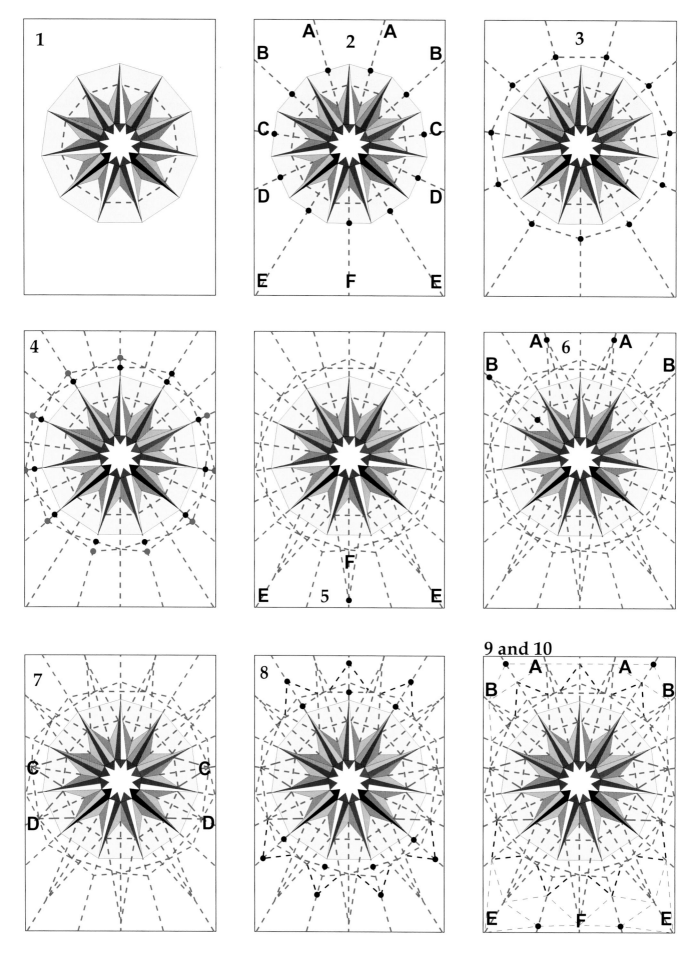

11

Layering and Quilting

The marking is complete. The next steps are to layer the banner, batting and backing.

Layering

The kit contains the batting already cut to size, eliminating this cutting step. If using a different batting, cut a piece of batting about 21" wide by 35" long.

Lay the background fabric saved for the back of the quilt wrong side up on the work surface and smooth it out. It measures about 36" long by 22" wide.

Place the batting on top of the backing. The batting should be a bit smaller than the backing so the raw edges of the backing can be seen. Trim the batting if necessary so the backing edges can be seen.

Lay the banner right side up on the backing/batting layers. Center it from side to side. The banner will be shorter than the backing so move it to approximately 2" from the top or bottom of the backing. Check to be sure that the sides of the backing are parallel to the sides of the banner. Smooth out the banner.

Using medium-size safety pins, pin through all three layers. Pin between the quilting lines so that the pins do not interfere with quilting. Add enough pins so that the layers are securely anchored and the layers will not shift when quilting.

Baste around the outside edges to keep them square and secure.

The three layers are ready for quilting.

Quilting

Machine or hand quilt on the marked lines. Begin sewing the quilting design near the center of the banner and work out toward the edges as quilting progresses. Stitch along the marked lines. In the process of quilting, stitch down the center of the Right and Left Wings and out to the edges of the banner.

Stitch down each side of the Outside Two-Color Star Point. Begin stitching in the ditch at the wide end, pivot at the star point and return to the wide end.

If machine quilting, at the beginning and end of each line take about four tiny stitches and on inside stops, leave a tail of about 4". Hide all thread tails by threading a needle and running the threads between fabric layers. Remove safety pins that are in the way of the machine presser foot or as quilting is completed in each area.

Quit around the edges of the logo if the logo design lends itself to that approach. Quilt 1/2" from the edge of the central hendecagon that contains the logo under the Inside Triangular Star Points. There is a quilting pattern for this area included with the pattern pieces at the back of this book. If no logo was used, there is an alternate quilting design for the center included with the patterns. Or select a design of your choice.

After quilting, the banner is ready for the addition of a hanging sleeve and binding.

Finishing

Trimming

The backing and batting are larger than the top and when the quilting is finished they need to be trimmed to the same size as the banner top.

Lay a straight edge along each side hold the straight edge securely and using the rotary cutter and mat, trim off the excess backing and batting. If a 12" x 12" square ruler is available or a 90 degree triangle, check in the process to see that the corners are square as the trimming progresses.

Sleeves

Refer to the cutting layout in the pattern section of this material (page 9). The sleeves are cut with the shortest measurement on the straight grain of the fabric.

1. Measure the width of the banner. Cut two sleeves 1/2" shorter than that measurement. For example, if the banner measures 20" wide, cut the sleeve 19-1/2" wide by the following measurements.

```
+-----------------------------+
|                             |
|                             |
|   Sleeve One = 6" x 19-1/2"  |
|                             |
|                             |
+-----------------------------+
```

Sleeve one is for the top of the banner and is cut 6" wide.

Sleeve two is for the bottom of the banner and is cut 3" wide by 19-1/2" long.

2. Fold the sleeves in half lengthwise right sides together. Pin 3" long ends together (or for sleeve two, the 1-1/2" side).

```
+-----------------------------+
| Sleeve One Folded in Half Lengthwise |
|        Size = 3" x 19-1/2"   |
+-----------------------------+
```

3. Sew a 1/4" seam in each end of both sleeves.

Sleeve One with 1/4" Seam at Each End

4. Turn the sleeves to the right side. Poke out corners. Match raw edges. Press, creasing the long folded edge.

```
+-----------------------------------------+
| S |                 Raw Edge          | S |
| e |                                   | e |
| a |                                   | a |
| m |  Fold                             | m |
+-----------------------------------------+
```
Sleeve One Turned to Right Side and Pressed
Size = 3" x 19"

5. Pin the raw edges of the top sleeve to the raw edge at the top of the banner back. Sleeve seam-end should be 1/2" from the banner raw edge.

The above steps are repeated for the narrower sleeve. The narrower sleeve is for the bottom of the banner. Match raw edges of the sleeve with the raw edges of the banner bottom. Pin in place and make sure bottom sleeve is 1/2" in from each edge of the banner side edges.

Binding

1. Refer to the fabric layout guide on page 9 and cut four strips 2" wide by 36" long. The length should be cut on the straight grain of the fabric. See illustrations on page 48.

2. Fold the wrong sides of the four strips together and press. They will measure 1" wide by the length from step one above.

3. Pin the raw edge of a binding strip to the raw edges of <u>right side</u> of the banner. Pin the sides first with about 4" of binding sticking out at the top and bottom.

4. Along the side of the banner and on the back of the banner, mark 1/4" from the top and bottom corners of the banner.

47

5. From the back, stitch the binding to the banner. Begin and end stitching 1/4" from the edge of the top and bottom. Back stitch at the beginning and end. It is easier to stitch on the back side of the banner because it is easier to see where to begin and end the stitching. Check periodically to be sure the binding raw edges are aligned with the banner raw edges.

6. The top and bottom binding is also pinned to the right side of the banner. There will be additional layers of fabric because of the sleeves. Sew the top and bottom binding in the same way the sides were sewn. Begin and end stitching at the point where the side binding stitching stopped.

7. Miter the corner binding edges. Directions are below.

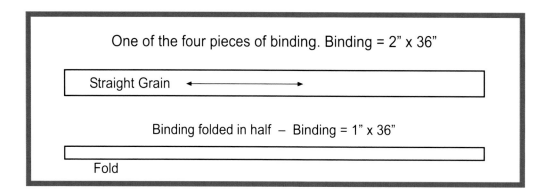

One of the four pieces of binding. Binding = 2" x 36"

Straight Grain ←——————→

Binding folded in half — Binding = 1" x 36"

Fold

Mitering

Mitering joins the side bindings to the top and bottom bindings and is relatively easy by following the directions on page 55. Only one corner is shown but all are done in the same way. The bindings are also shown lighter in color to help highlight them. In this project, the bindings are the same color as the background and backing.

Mark the miters on the back side of the binding so marks will not show on the right side. However, use a water soluble blue marking pen for this process or a white marking pencil.

Complete the other three corners using the same mitering steps. When the mitering is finished, turn the binding to the back of the banner. Gently fold the mitered corners right side out. Gently extend the points being careful not to poke sharp pointed objects through the fabric or hyperextend the corners. Flatten the corners of the banner under the miters.

Pin the binding to the back of the banner. Stitch the binding to the back of the banner using an invisible hand stitch. The sleeves will be loose at this point.

Note: An invisible stitch in achieved by passing the needle into the fold of the binding, where the fold forms a little tunnel, taking a small stitch and pulling the needle and thread back out. The needle is placed in the backing right across from where it came out of the binding and just outside the binding seam line and another similar stitch is taken in the

back. These stitches are all kept small and periodically, the thread is drawn taut.

A good reference for this stitch is in the book *Invisible Appliqué* by Ami Simms.

Below is an illustration of the finished banner quilted and bound. The sleeves need to be stitched to the back.

The quilted banner is bound.
The binding fold is stitched to the back.

48

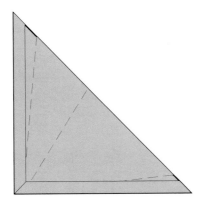

This is a close-up of the bottom left corner

Sleeves

Move the top sleeve up and away from the banner back so that it sticks out past the binding seam line.

Fold it down toward the banner back so that the fold of the sleeve aligns with the bound top edge of the banner top. The fold should not be visible beyond the binding. Pin the bottom edge of the sleeve to the back of the quilt. This folding process creates a pleat at the top of the sleeve which allows the banner to hang with out puckering.

Stitch the pinned sleeve edge to the back of the banner using an invisible stitch. Be sure that the stitches do not show on the front of the banner.

Do not sew the bottom sleeve down yet.

Bottom Weights

The bottom sleeve is for the rope drapery weights. Place the length of weights at the seam line of the bottom sleeve where it meets the binding seam line. Turn the ends of the rope weights in to prevent their cloth casing from raveling. Loosely whip-stitch the weights in place.

Fold the bottom sleeve in the same way that the top sleeve was folded, covering the rope weights. Pin the sleeve down and then stitch it down using an invisible stitch.

Blue Water Soluble Quilting Line Markings

The blue markings are removed by completely submerging the banner in water. It is best to place the banner in a bath tub so it can lay flat. Run cool water into the tub and place the banner in the water.

The blue marks will disappear. Swish the banner around, drain water and rinse again. This process also removes the starch. Roll the banner in a terry cloth towel to remove most of the water.

Blocking

Block the banner to keep it square while drying. Blocking is done by pinning the banner to a Styrofoam board. Check to be sure banner is square and measurements are equal as straight pins are added. Let it dry on the board. Press lightly after it is dry.

Rod

Insert a decorative rod in the top of the banner. Add the decorative hanging cord. Add a tassel to each side if desired.

University Pins

Consider two locations for displaying the pins. Page 6 shows the pins around the center hendecagon on the Inside Triangular Star Points. On the book cover and on page 50, they are shown placed at the star points outside the hendecagon unit on the quilted background.

The size of the pins collected will influence placement. Select one of these two locations and insert the university pins. Any other location can also be selected. Add the pin back to lock them in place.

Many pins are lapel or tie tack size and have a push on back but there are a variety of pin sizes to select from. Collecting pins is a fun part of this project. A set of pins can be ordered. Send an e-mail with your request to: starandlogobanner@comcast.net. There is also an Order Form on the last page of this book.

**The drawing below of the finished banner
includes pictures of the university pins.**

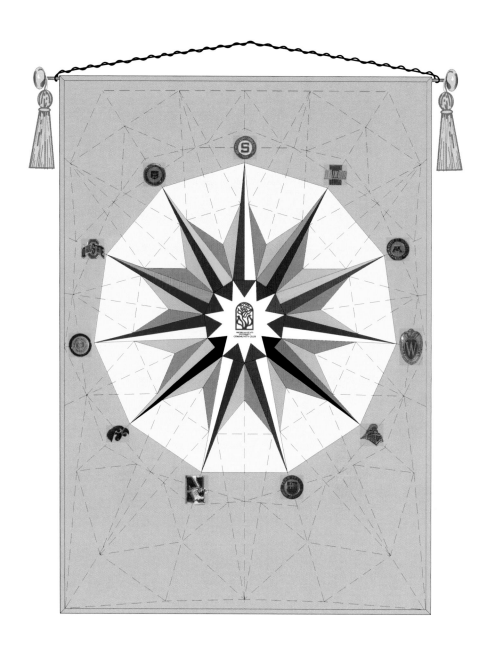

Bonus Pages

Tie Tacking Directions

Mitering Binding Directions

and

**Pattern Pieces to Use for
Cutting Fabric and
Marking Fabric**

Tie Tacking

The Eleven-Step Process

Defined

Tie Tacking is the process of tying two points together with thread instead of pinning.

Consider two pieces of fabric. Both have a place that is to be matched where the two pieces are going to be brought together. These can be a set of crossing seams or two points that are to flow smoothly from one section to another. Eventually a seam will be sewn to join the two pieces of fabric. This process can also apply to matching repeats on print or plaid fabrics so the seam becomes almost invisible.

Rationale

Why use Tie Tacking? When two points are matched using a straight pin, the process of rotating the pin to anchor it in the fabric, shifts the layers and the point is matched better than not pinning at all but not as good as can be achieved by Tie Tacking.

Initially it seems as though Tie Tacking takes more time, but this method often saves time because it is more accurate than using pins. The shift of fabric when using pins can lead to pulling out stitches and to re-doing the sewing. Many quilters have had this happen.

When there is a goal to match points precisely the first time, Tie Tacking has it over pinning every time and is then more productive. With most sewing projects, where precision is needed, use Tie Tacking.

Preparation

Thread a sewing needle with a neutral color thread or one that matches the fabrics being joined. Use either regular sewing thread or button/craft thread. Use a double strand of sewing thread or a single strand of button/craft thread, which is heavier.

Place a good sized knot in the end of the thread.

Below is a picture of two red and green on white background star blocks. They are sitting on a black surface. Star points can be difficult to match accurately. The Tie Tacking process helps ensure a match on the first attempt.

The Tie Tacking steps to the star point matching process follow.

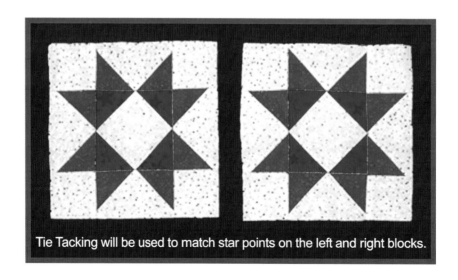

Tie Tacking will be used to match star points on the left and right blocks.

Process

Black thread is used to demonstrate.

1. From the wrong side of the first piece of fabric, poke the needle through the point to be matched. Check the right side of the fabric to be sure the needle came through at the correct spot.

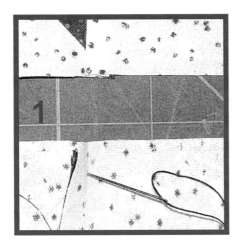

2. Pull the thread through until the knot is against the wrong side of the fabric.

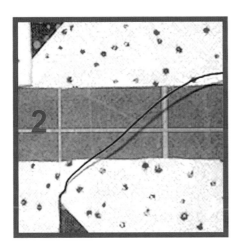

3. Pick up the second piece of fabric and poke the needle through the right side of the fabric into the point that is to be matched.

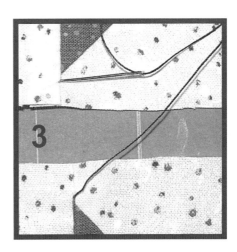

4. From the back of the second fabric, poke the needle through to the right side so that you have made a tiny stitch in the back. The needle should be very near the first needle hole but not in the exact hole. If it is in the same hole, the thread will come out.

5. Pull the needle with thread through but leave the thread slack. The fabric pieces will be hanging loose. Later steps bring the two pieces together and then the thread is tightened.

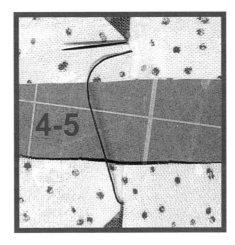

6. On the right side, poke the needle into the point on the first piece of fabric. Place the needle very near the original needle hole but not exactly in it. See photo 6 on page 54.

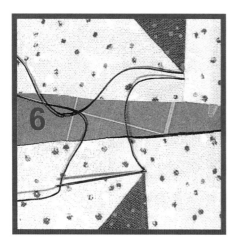

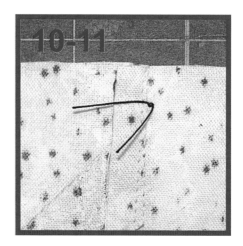

7. Pull the needle and thread through to the wrong side of fabric one.

8. Pull the two pieces of fabric together by pulling the thread and bringing the two layers of fabric together.

9. Pull the knot away from the fabric leaving about a 3" tail.

Repeat this sewing sequence when matching additional points.

In the photo below, the center seam has not yet been sewn but upon opening the two pieces, you can see that the points match. The red circles show the two points that were drawn together using the Tie Tack method.

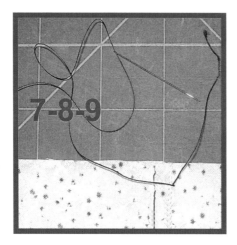

10. Tie the needle end and knot end together like a knot in a pair of shoe laces would be done. Tighten it snugly and tie a second and third knot tightly to secure the connection.

11. Trim off the threads leaving a small tail. Now that the two places being matched are Tie Tacked, the fabric can be moved, rotated, pinned in other places and the point positions will not change. This process reduces the pins needed and makes seam sewing much easier.

See the top right photo that shows completed steps 10 and 11.

The next step would be to turn the fabric to the wrong side, pin raw edges and sew the seam.

Compare the photo at the beginning of this process to the one above to get a before and after glimpse.

Mitering Binding

Below is a 1/8 scale illustration of the 20" x 28" banner. It has the bindings added. The binding sticks out 3" to 4" beyond the raw edge of the quilt on all sides. The top and bottom borders are folded away from the quilt and the side borders are folded toward the front of the quilt. For illustrative purposes, only the top left corner of the quilt will be shown in the binding steps that follow. This area is circled in red as seen below. The bindings are shown in a lighter color to define them but would match the background color.

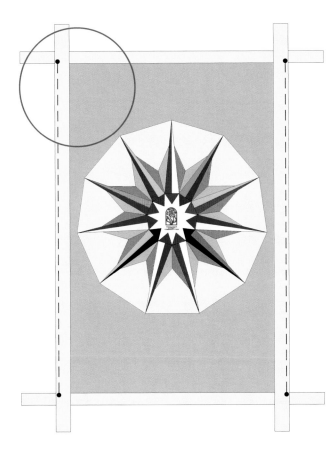

1. Fold top binding up away from banner. As shown above.

2. Fold the side binding toward the banner. Which is also shown above.

Be sure both bindings lay flat.

Steps 1 and 2 are illustrated above in the scaled drawing.

3. Lay a straight edge along seam line of top binding so that it crosses the side binding.

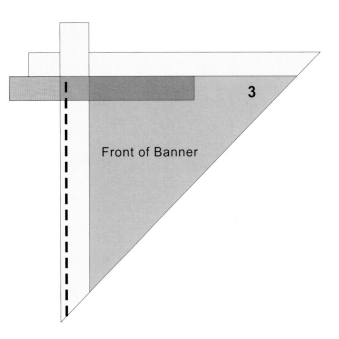

4. Place a small dot on side binding fold where straight edge crosses binding fold.

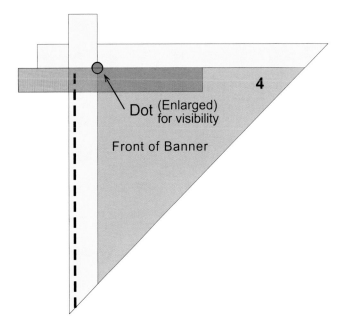

55

5. Fold the side binding out away from banner.

6. Fold the top binding toward banner front.

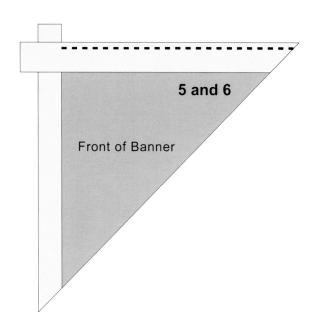

5 and 6

Front of Banner

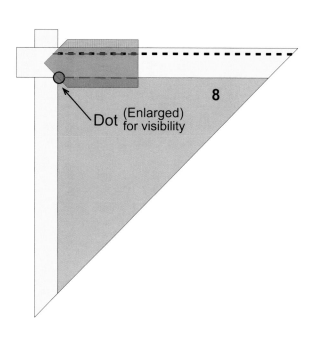

Dot (Enlarged) for visibility

8

9. Draw a line along the 45 degree side of the ruler from the dot to just past the center of the binding.

7. As in step 4, place small a dot on the top binding fold where the straight edge crosses binding fold.

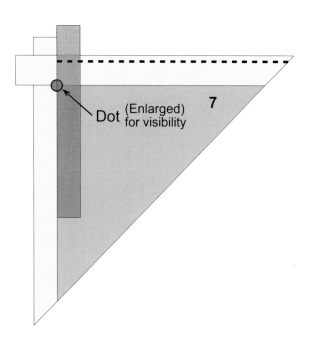

Dot (Enlarged) for visibility

7

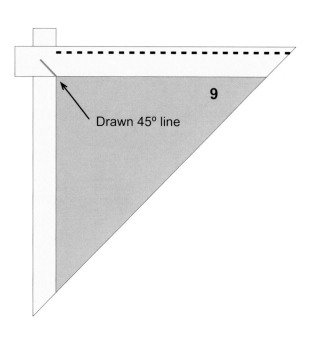

Drawn 45° line

9

10. The Corner Mark-It ruler 45 degree side is moved to the stopping point of the stitching line.

The ruler straight edges are aligned with the binding fold and raw edges.

8. Utilizing the Corner Mark-It ruler, lay the pointed 45 degree angle at the dot on the binding.

Align Corner Mark-It straight edges with the binding fold, seam stitching line and raw edges of the binding.

Another 45 degree line is drawn from the stitching stopping point and needs to cross the first one drawn from the dot at the fold.

There will be an arrow-like shape formed by the two lines.

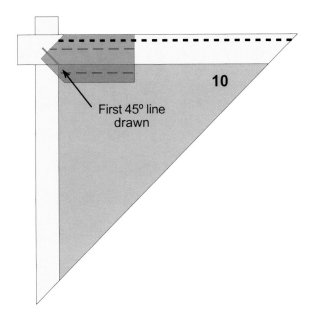

First 45° line
drawn

10

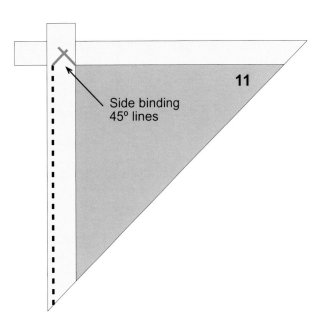

Side binding
45° lines

11

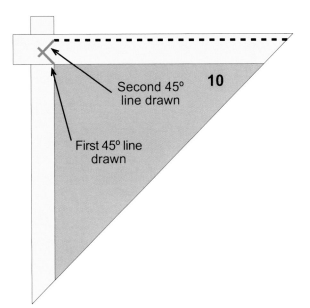

Second 45°
line drawn

10

First 45° line
drawn

11. This 45 degree marking process is repeated for the side binding. Illustration 11 shows the end result.

Repeat the above eleven steps on all four corners, two markings on each corner for a total of eight arrow-like markings.

12. Bring the top binding and side binding together and align the dots. Fold the banner out of the way. Pin the bindings together temporarily.

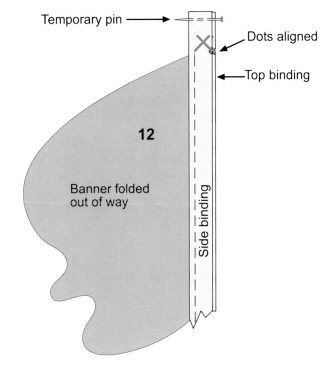

Temporary pin

Dots aligned

Top binding

12

Banner folded
out of way

Side binding

13. Use a thread color that matches binding fabric and thread a needle, knot the thread and bring the needle point from the wrong side of the binding through to the dot at the fold edge of the binding. Keep the needle between the two layers of fabric that make up the binding. The thread should not show on the right side of the binding. Here the thread is shown in black for clarity.

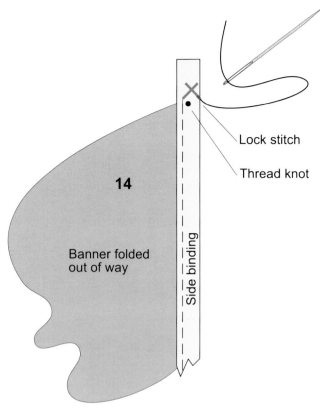

Lock stitch

Thread knot

14

Banner folded out of way

Side binding

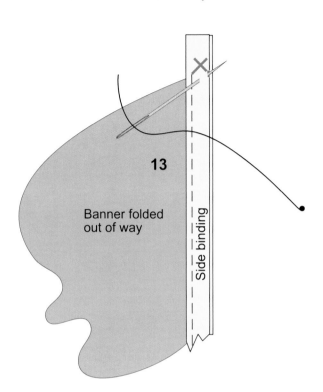

13

Banner folded out of way

Side binding

15. Pin through the side and top binding fabric layers at the point where the blue 45 degree lines cross.

14. Take a lock stitch at the very edge of the side and top bindings by the dots. This prevents the fabric from puckering when the thread between the knot and edge of the binding is pulled tight.

For this lock stitch, bring the needle and thread through the dot with the knot against the binding as shown.

Next, take a small stitch through the dot on the top binding and snug the two dots against each other.

Take a tiny overcast stitch catching both binding folds in it. Loop the thread over the needle. Pull the thread up tight, creating a fine locking stitch at the fold of the binding. Take it in the direction of the 45 degree blue line. The thread knot (shown in black) and lock stitch (shown in red) are exaggerated.

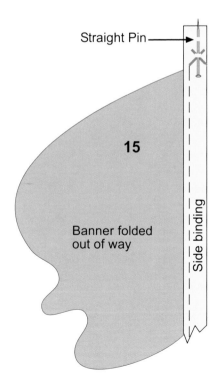

Straight Pin

15

Banner folded out of way

Side binding

16. By hand take tiny running stitches from the dot at the fold along the 45 degree line and up toward the point where the two 45 degree lines cross. Check periodically to be sure the marking lines on the top binding align with those on the side binding. Remove the pin before reaching the crossing point. Back stitch periodically. Be sure your stitches are going through all layers of the binding fabric.

Take a backstitch at the point where the two marking lines cross. Pivot the needle and stitch toward the seam line of the binding. Back stitch at the seam line, pivot the needle and stitch again toward where the two blue lines cross. Using a tiny whipstitch, knot off before reaching the crossing point.

17. Trim off the binding layers outside the stitching line. Leave slightly more than an 1/8" of fabric beyond stitching.

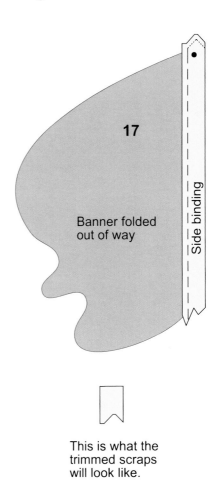

This is what the trimmed scraps will look like.

Repeat steps 12 through 17 on all four corners.

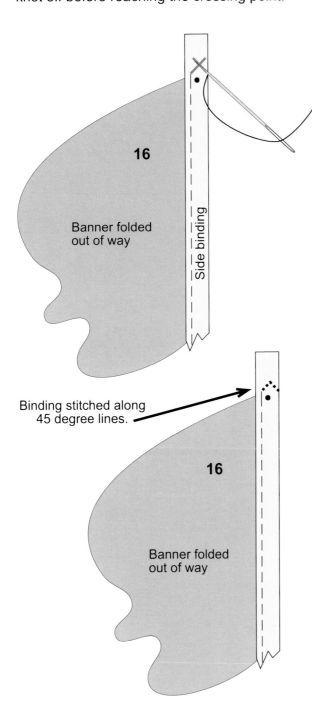

Binding stitched along 45 degree lines.

59

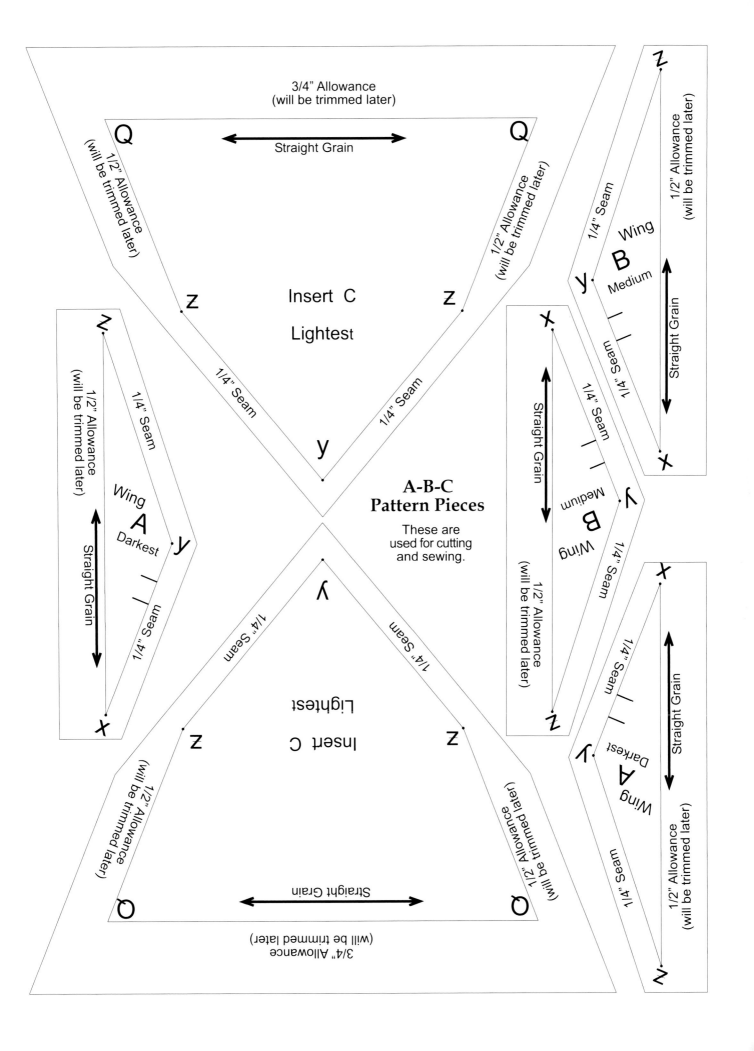

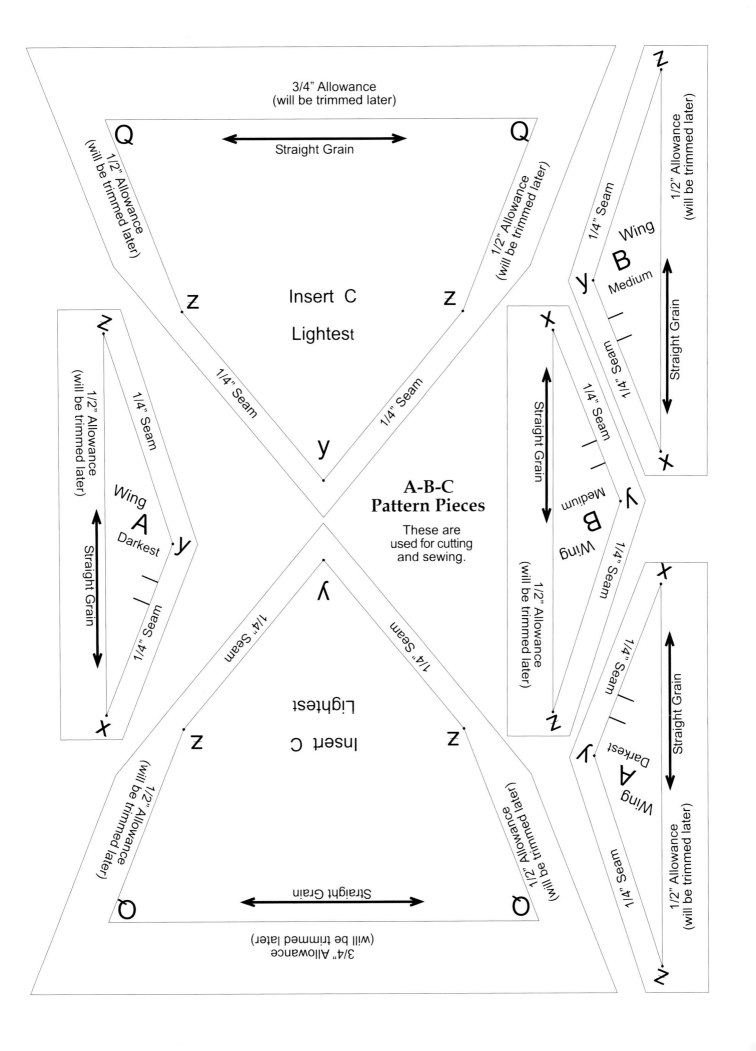

A-B-C
Pattern Pieces

These are
used for cutting
and sewing.

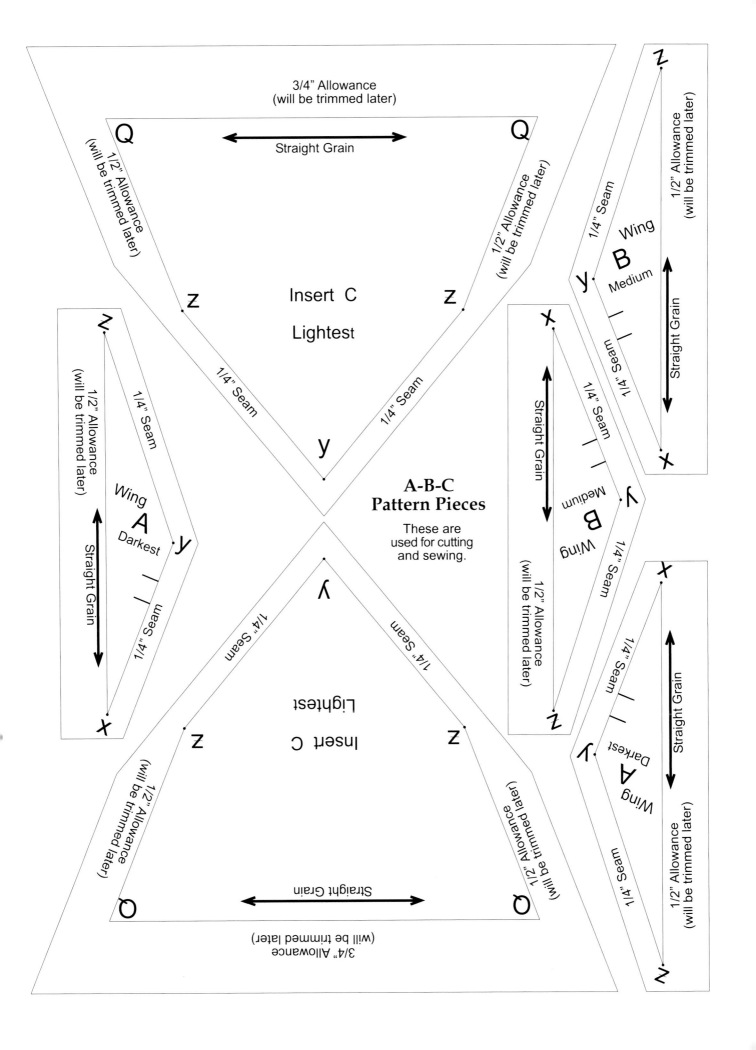

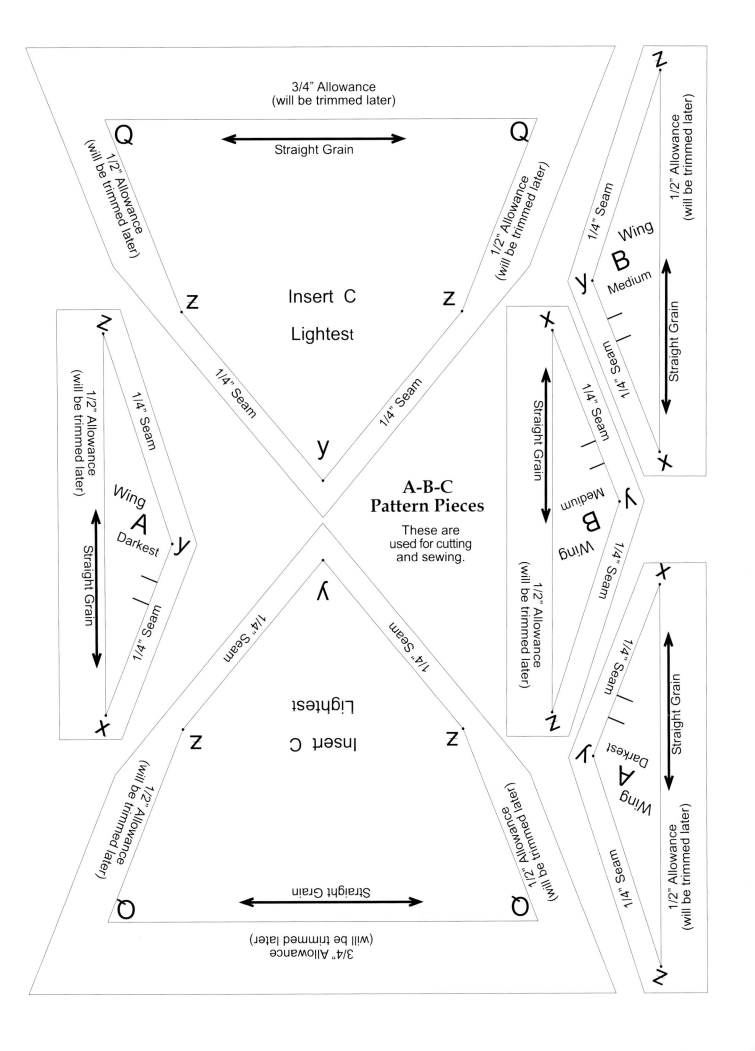

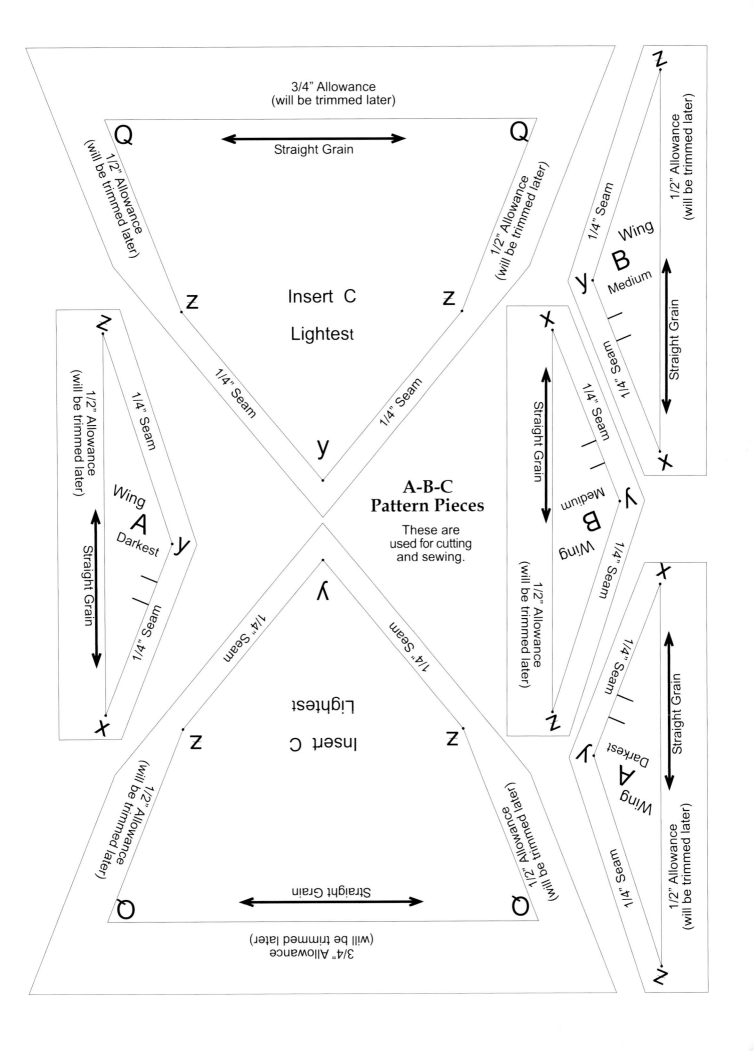

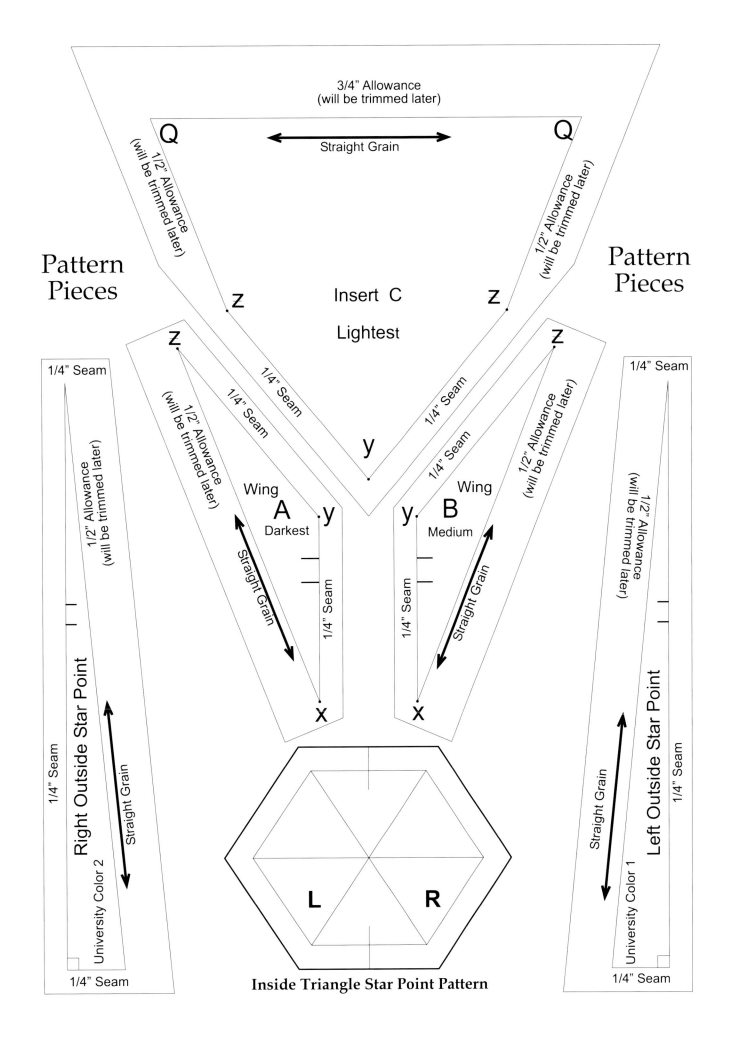

Pattern Pieces

Pattern Pieces

3/4" Allowance
(will be trimmed later)

Q
Q
Straight Grain

1/2" Allowance
(will be trimmed later)

1/2" Allowance
(will be trimmed later)

z
z

z
Z

Insert C

Lightest

1/4" Seam
1/4" Seam
1/4" Seam

1/4" Seam
1/4" Seam
1/4" Seam

1/4" Seam

1/4" Seam

1/2" Allowance
(will be trimmed later)

1/2" Allowance
(will be trimmed later)

1/2" Allowance
(will be trimmed later)

1/2" Allowance
(will be trimmed later)

y

Wing
A
Darkest
y

y
B
Wing
Medium

1/4" Seam

1/4" Seam

Straight Grain

Straight Grain

x
x

Right Outside Star Point

Left Outside Star Point

University Color 2

University Color 1

Straight Grain

Straight Grain

1/4" Seam

1/4" Seam

1/4" Seam

1/4" Seam

L
R

Inside Triangle Star Point Pattern

Straight Grain

3/4" Allowance
(will be trimmed later)

Q   Q

1/2" Allowance
(will be trimmed later)

1/2" Allowance
(will be trimmed later)

A-B-C Pattern Checker

1. Trim paper from along both lines Y/Z so that just the pattern lines show. This pattern will be used to determine if any sewing adjustments are needed after sewing unit A-B-C together.

2. This pattern should fit accurately into the V-groove made after sewing Wings A and B to Insert C. Pin pattern in place. If the seam lines do not match up to this pattern, adjust the seams by taking either A or B off and moving the fabric over to meet the pattern. Pin adjusted side in place and re-sew seam. Check again.

Z   Z

Insert C

Checker and Trimmer Page

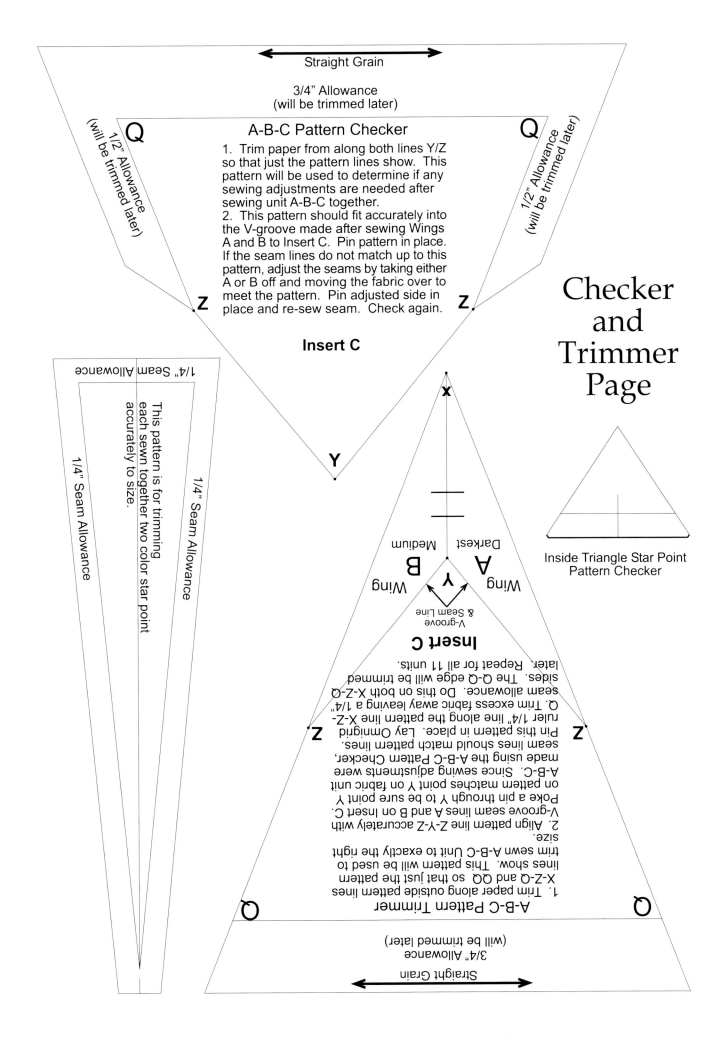

Inside Triangle Star Point
Pattern Checker

X

Y

Medium   Darkest

Wing **B**   Y   Wing **A**

V-groove & Seam Line

Insert C

1/4" Seam Allowance

1/4" Seam Allowance

This pattern is for trimming each sewn together two color star point accurately to size.

1/4" Seam Allowance

A-B-C Pattern Trimmer

1. Trim paper along outside pattern lines X-Z-Q and QQ so that just the pattern lines show. This pattern will be used to trim sewn A-B-C Unit to exactly the right size.

2. Align pattern line Z-Y-Z accurately with V-groove seam lines A and B on Insert C. Poke a pin through Y to be sure point Y on pattern matches point Y on fabric unit A-B-C. Since sewing adjustments were made using the A-B-C Pattern Checker, seam lines should match pattern lines. Pin this pattern in place. Lay Omnigrid ruler 1/4" line along the pattern line X-Z-Q. Trim excess fabric away leaving a 1/4" seam allowance. Do this on both X-Z-Q sides. The Q-Q edge will be trimmed later. Repeat for all 11 units.

Q   Q

3/4" Allowance
(will be trimmed later)

Straight Grain

Center Hendecagon Pattern

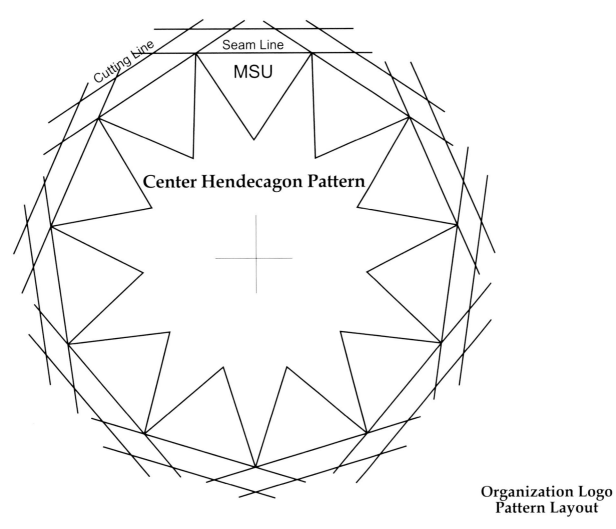

Cutting Line

Seam Line

MSU

Center Hendecagon Pattern

MSU

Full Size Center Hendecagon Quilting Pattern

(See directions for using this pattern in the section on marking the quilting design.)

+

Quilt around your logo which is inside this quilting outline.

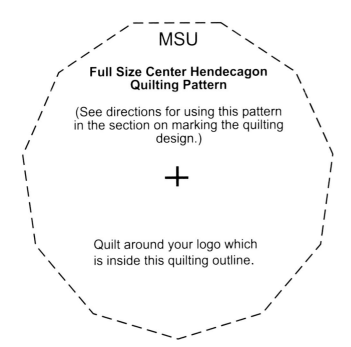

Organization Logo Pattern Layout

On 8-1/2" x 11"
Fabric Printer Sheet

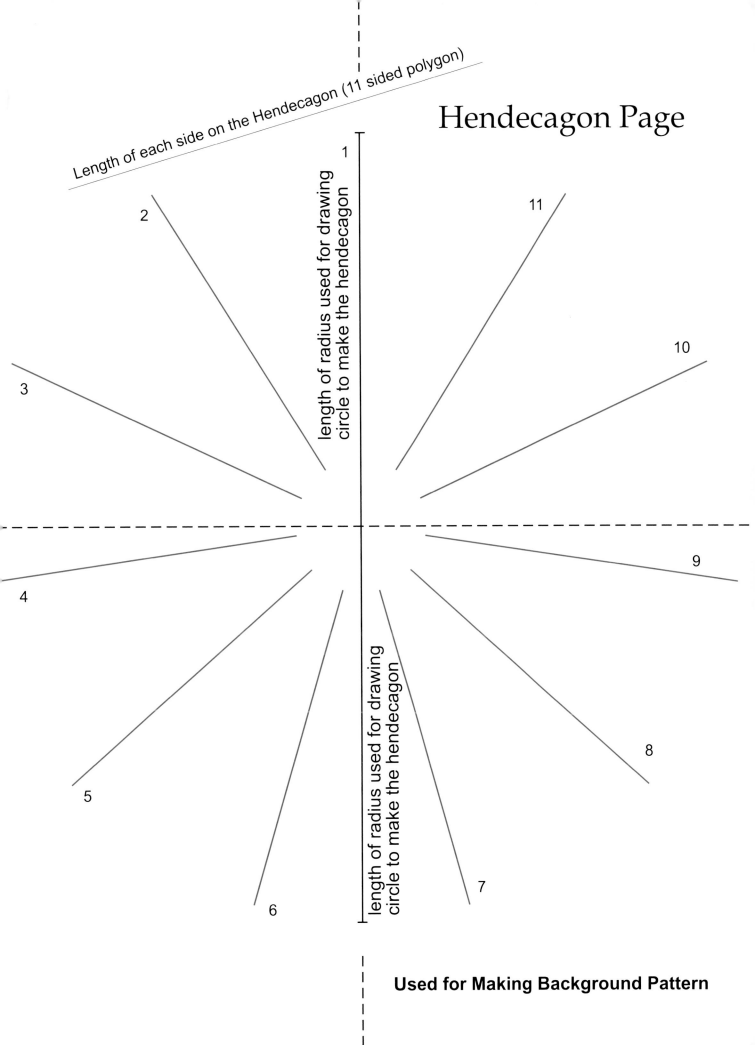

Length of each side on the Hendecagon (11 sided polygon)

Hendecagon Page

length of radius used for drawing circle to make the hendecagon

1

2

11

3

10

4

9

length of radius used for drawing circle to make the hendecagon

5

8

6

7

Used for Making Background Pattern

Order Form

**Give the gift of the Quilted Star and Logo Banner book,
fabric kit or pin collection
to your friends and colleagues.**

☐   Yes, I would like to place an order.

Name_____

Address _____

_____

City/State/Zip _____

Phone _____
(Will phone **only** if there are questions about your order.)

E-mail _____

Ordered by _____

Packages will not be shipped to a P.O. Box address or to foreign countries.

.SHIP TO (if different from address above)

Name_____

Address_____

_____

City/State/Zip_____

┌─────────────────────┐
│   Fill in order   │
│ information on   │
│ reverse side of   │
│   this form.   │
└─────────────────────┘

Full—(Circle)—Publications

1261 Cambria Drive
East Lansing, MI 48823-2388

starandlogobanner@comcast.net

Order Form

ITEM #	DESCRIPTION	PRICE EACH	HOW MANY?	TOTAL
BB 2008	**Quilted Star and Logo Banner book:** For Organizations and Individuals with a Big Ten Affiliation, And Anyone Interested in Making an Eleven-Point Star Where Each Point has Two Colors	$21.95		
CFK 2008	**Companion fabric kits:** Kit contains all fabrics needed to make Quilted Star and Logo banner/wall hanging, fabric printer sheet and batting—washed and ready to use	$47.95		
BTP 2008	**Big Ten university pin collection:** Collection contains all eleven Big Ten university lapel pins to complete the banner/wall hanging.	$65.95		
BFPC 2008	**Book, fabric kit and pin collection:** Boxed and ready for gift giving	$122.95		
SP 2009	**Spirit pin:** Be part of the whole! Pin features the book's 11-point star design - a full-color 1-1/4" lapel pin.	$9.95		
MBS 2009	**Magnetic bumper sticker:** Features a full-color 11-point star design and words: "Part of he Whole." (4" x 12")	$4.95		
S 2009	**T-shirt or polo shirt:** Visit www.full-circle-publications.com for available designs, sizing and prices.			
			Merchandise total	
1.				
2. Michigan shipments add 6% sales tax to above total				
3. Shipping: see chart at left and add here				
			TOTAL: (add lines 1, 2 and 3)	

Standard Shipping

Standard Shipping			Standard Shipping		
Up to $25.00	Add	$ 5.00	$125.01 - $150.00	Add	$ 15.00
$25.01 - $50.00	Add	$ 7.00	$150.01 - $175.00	Add	$ 17.00
$50.00 - $75.00	Add	$ 9.00	$175.01 - $200.00	Add	$ 19.00
$75.01 - $100.00	Add	$ 11.00	$200.01 - $225.00	Add	$ 21.00
$100.01 - $125.00	Add	$ 13.00	over $225.01	Add	10% of total order

[ ] My check or money order for $_____ is enclosed.

Allow two weeks for delivery.

Payment must accompany order. Make your check payable and return to:

Full—Circle—Publications

1261 Cambria Drive
East Lansing, MI 48823-2388

e-mail questions to: starandlogobanner@comcast.net

Visit: **www.full-circle-publications.com**

Fill in shipping information on reverse side of this form.